Talking Dirty –

In Yiddish?

Ilene Schneider

Aakenbaaken & Kent New York

Talking Dirty - In Yiddish?

Aakenbaaken & Kent   New York

aakenbaakeneditor@gmail.com

Author photograph by Jaclyn Savits of Savitz Photography

ISBN: 978-1-938436-20-8

the shadiest hospital in New England. This is Schneider's best yet.

Robert Lopresti,   Award-winning author of *Greenfellas*

Yom Killer is a heartwarming tale of murder and Medicare fraud.

Jeff Markowitz, Author of the *Casey O'Malley Mysteries* and of *Death and White Diamonds*

When I finished the last of the twelve Rabbi David Small mysteries (That Day The Rabbi Left Town), I experienced the sense of loss anyone who enjoys series feels when there is not a next one. Now, twenty years later, I have discovered the Rabbi Aviva Cohen series. The David Small character was rabbi for an orthodox congregation. Aviva Cohen's congregation is not orthodox, and no one would describe her as orthodox, religiously or otherwise. Rabbi Aviva Cohen is brash, funny, nosy, and blunt. In a word, *meshuganah*. But she is every bit as captivating and the mysteries every bit as much fun as Kemelman's work, the first of which won an Edgar. Maybe Rabbi Ilene Schneider will win one as well. From my lips to G*d's ear, I can hear her saying.

Mike Orenduff, Author of the award-winning *Pot Thief Murder Mysteries*

A heroine who loves Mel Brooks, Milky Ways and matzoh balls - what's not to love? Rabbi Aviva Cohen is back in action trading quips with her quirky relatives and besting bad guys when a series of mysterious deaths at a senior facility strikes perilously close to home. Great fun - and as the saying goes "you don't have to be Jewish..." Rosemary Harris, Author of the Anthony and Agatha-nominated *Pushing Up Daisies* and *The Bitches of Brooklyn*

Chanukah Guilt

Lots of fun! - *Midwest Book Review*

Wonderful well-written characters will pull you in. - *Armchair Interviews*

A well-crafted story and a satisfying conclusion. - *Muse Reviews*

Will be enjoyed by our readers. - South Florida Association of Jewish Libraries

Weaves Jewish culture and mystery in a delightful blend. I enjoyed this cozy mystery and look forward to the next installment by this talented author. - *Bloodstained Book Reviews*

Bravo Ilene Schneider! Chanukah Guilt is a grand success! I can't wait for more Rabbi Cohen! -*My Shelf*

Schneider succeeds in blending the complex life of a congregational spiritual leader with that of first-rate detective, family member, confidant,

friend, human being and even yenta (nosy body).
- *San Diego Jewish World*

Unleavened Dead

A solid, funny mystery that provides an insider's look at Jewish life. -*Ellery Queen Mystery Magazine*

As always, Schneider gives us a wonderful picture of life in a Jewish community - Chaim Potok with a wacky sense of humor. - Donna Fletcher Crow, A *Darkly Hidden Truth, The Monastery Murders 2*

Oy vey, this book made me smile … Unleavened Dead is a book you don't want to miss. - Barb Goffman, Agatha, Anthony, and Macavity award-nominated author.

Rabbi Aviva Cohen is funny, smart, and believable … A smoothly written and entirely enjoyable read! - Sheila Connolly, Agatha Award nominated author of the *Orchard Mysteries* and the *Museum Mysteries*.

Like dishing with your girlfriend the rabbi, who leads a really interesting life. - Kate Gallison, author of *The Edge of Ruin* (as Irene Fleming), winner of the New Jersey Studies Academic Alliance fiction award

Once again, the inimitable Aviva Cohen uses her rabbinic seichel and intuition to solve crime ... This is a delightful cozy mystery for everyone! - Deborah Shlian, co-author of the award winning *Sammy Greene* series

Aviva is a great character, full of fun, somebody you'd feel comfortable hanging out with. Even though there are many mentions of Jewish tradition, non-Jews won't feel bombarded with too much information or miss any good clues along the way. - Sandra Murphy, *Kings River Life*

Schneider has given us a plot that has just the right amount of complexities, interesting characters to both love and hate, enough twists to keep us guessing throughout the story, and a Jewish holiday setting that adds to the stress. I can wholeheartedly recommend this novel. - Davida Chazan, *Yahoo Reviews*

I loved every page of this book. Ilene Schneider has a light hand with the humor, lots of puns and jokes, but also depth and layers and passion to her characters, even minor ones. - Dawn Roberto, *LR&M Reviews*

Unleavened Dead is the second book in the Rabbi Cohen mystery series and one that I thoroughly enjoyed. It is a quick, easy read and a good mystery without the graphic violence of some of the better known mystery authors. I thoroughly recommend this book to all lovers of the mystery genre. - *Night Owl Suspense*

I felt pulled into a whole new world. The plot was interesting and the characters unique. I liked this story from the beginning to the end."
Michelle Perin, Chair of Award Committee, Public Safety Writers Association

Dedication

This book is dedicated to all those who spoke the rich, colorful, dynamic language known as Yiddish, and to those who are committed to keeping the language just as alive and vibrant today.

Table of Contents

Forward

This book will not teach you how to speak Yiddish. Instead, it will introduce - or reintroduce - you to various idiomatic phrases and colloquial vocabulary words that can be sprinkled in your conversation to enrich and enliven it, to give it some texture and interest.

In addition, the words are not just listed by subject matter and then translated. There are mini-essays scattered among the definitions that add a sociological and historical context to the vocabulary. The information will help non-Jews understand the milieu in which Yiddish developed and flourished, and contains some little known facts and trivia to interest knowledgeable readers.

It has been my intention to present a book that is both informative and entertaining, without being either too academic or too superficial. I hope I have succeeded.

Note from the editor: Yiddish words that have been adopted into English or are widely understood by English speakers are not italicized. Since "widely understood" is a subjective term, readers may disagree with the use of italics in this book.

Introduction

Talking dirty - in Yiddish? I always thought it could not be done, that there are curses but not curse words in Yiddish. But Yiddish does have vulgarisms, coarse language, colorful insults, and offensive words. It even has the equivalent of four-letter Anglo-Saxon "expletive deleted" words. This book will teach you how to use them all - but will not guarantee that you will still have any friends afterwards.

Shortly after being asked to write this book, I was at a conference attended by several Yiddish speakers and mentioned the project to some I met. Their universal reaction was: "How to talk dirty in Yiddish? Can't be done." My informants were all women "of a certain age" and professional Yiddishists and linguists. When I mentioned the topic of the book to casual Yiddish speakers, I found out it can be done, but not in public.

As one woman at the conference explained to me, "Who did I learn Yiddish from? My mother. She'd never use such words. So I don't know any. Well, there is *Lig in drerd*, but that's all." The phrase means literally, "Lay in the ground" or "Drop dead." Not exactly dirty, but as dirty as she had ever heard.

Another woman at the conference agreed: "My mother had sex once. That's how I got born. When she went to the gynecologist, she described her symptoms as being *dorten*, 'down there.'" She did provide me with two examples, however: *Gai kak'n in dem yam*, literally "Go shit in the ocean," or "Get lost;" and *Gai tren zich*, or "Go fuck yourself." I suspect that she was embarrassed that she knew these phrases, and was probably worried her mother would rise up from the grave to wash her mouth out with soap.

Someone else told me the only dirty word she could think of (and it was in English) was cancer. The word was always referred to obliquely, in hushed tones. "Did you hear? He has you-know-what."

But what they did not consider was that words like shiksa (a non-Jewish woman) or *shaigitz* (a non-Jewish man) could be perceived as offensive. To many Yiddish speakers, these words are merely descriptive, but there is an implication of distain that make them as taboo as drek (shit).

The word drek is illustrative of the transformation that occurred when many Yiddish words and phrases made their way into English. These words became innocuous replacements for the equivalent Anglo-Saxon words. Lenny Bruce is credited with having brought these words into the mainstream of English usage when he realized that the censors, who would have him kicked off the stage for saying "prick," not to mention what they would have done to his TV show (canceled it), had no idea that shmuck meant the same thing.

For example, in his book, *Jewhooing the Sixties: American Celebrity and Jewish Identity*, David Kaufman quotes one of Bruce's routines about how he was arrested on an obscenity charge by an undercover Yiddish-speaking agent who was "placed in the club to determine if Bruce's constant use of Yiddish terms was a cover for profanity. The officer said it was."

Of all the words and phrases in this book, about sixty are considered "impolite" and only about twenty-five of those are considered truly obscene. (George Carlin was able to identify a measly seven in English). But I would not recommend using them or the other thirty-five rude words in polite society ... unless you want your mother to wash your mouth out with soap.

Background Information

I. What is Yiddish Anyway?

The etymology of the word "Yiddish" goes back to the Latin word for Jew, from *Iudaeus*, someone from the Roman territory of Judah. From there it developed into the Old High German word *judo*, and thence to the Middle High German word *jüdisch*, from *jude*, German for Jew. Even though it was not known by the Yiddish word *yidish* until 1875, the language began to develop in Central Europe in the Ninth Century. From the Twelfth Century on, it was referred to as Lashon Ashkenaz, the language of the Ashkenaz.

In many ways, it is easier to examine what Yiddish is not. It is not Hebrew. It is not German written in Hebrew letters. It is not the lingua Franca of the Jewish people. It is not a dead language.

In actuality, it is all of those things to some extent, but with exceptions, explanations, and a lot of "yes, but" qualifying statements.

It is not Hebrew. Yes, but . . . it does have a lot of Hebrew words, although pronounced differently from the Modern Hebrew of Israel. Shabbos, for example, is the Yiddish-inflected Eastern European pronunciation for Shabbat, the Sabbath. *Yontif* (pronounced with a short-o and short-i), the word for holiday, is *Yom Tov* (both words with a long-o) in Hebrew. Many other words have a Hebrew etymology. Tuchus, buttocks, for example, is from the Hebrew *takhat*, under.

There are two different pronunciations of Hebrew - Ashkenazi and Sephardi. Ashkenaz was the name given to Central Europe, dominated by Germany. The plural noun Ashkenazim became generalized to apply to all Jews of Central or Eastern European descent, as opposed to the Sephardim, those who could trace their origins to the Iberian Peninsula before they were expelled from there by the Inquisition in 1492. With some exceptions, Ashkenazim came from Christian countries and Sephardim from Moslem ones.

Settling in Moslem countries that spoke Arabic or other Semitic languages, the Sephardim retained what is considered to be the original pronunciation of Hebrew. The Hebrew pronunciation used by Ashkenazim changed over the centuries of living in the midst of a general population that spoke Teutonic or Slavic languages. The emphasis shifted from the last to the first syllable, and the pronunciation of certain hard consonants became soft, with, for example, the final "t" becoming "s."

When Hebrew was revived as the official language of Israel, the Sephardi pronunciation was adopted, although more traditionally religious Israelis from Central and Eastern Europe have retained the Ashkenazi pronunciation for prayer and study. Today, the Sephardi pronunciation is standard in the United States in almost all but Orthodox synagogues.

From yivo.com:

"The YIVO Institute for Jewish Research was founded as the Jewish Scientific Institute in Vilna, Poland in 1925, by scholars, teachers, and other communal activists who saw the Yiddish language as the best medium for educating the Jewish population, and of giving the Jewish people access to their history and culture. The institution they developed produced groundbreaking scholarship in Yiddish and published scholarly journals, but also organized popular lectures, exhibitions, cultural evenings, and training seminars for teachers in Yiddish primary schools and high schools.

"YIVO became the acknowledged authority on the Yiddish language and pioneered important linguistic research on Yiddish. The standards YIVO developed for Yiddish orthography, or spelling, and for the transliteration of Yiddish into English are the most commonly used by publishers and scholars. YIVO's Modern English-Yiddish Yiddish-English Dictionary, first published in 1968, has now appeared in several editions.

"YIVO continues to serve as the 'world headquarters' of the Yiddish language. Hundreds of students have attended its weekly Yiddish language courses or graduated from its intensive summer Yiddish program."

It is not German written in Hebrew letters. Yes, but . . . it is a Teutonic language, although a separate one from German. According to the website of the Institute for Jewish Research (yivo.com), one theory of the origin of Yiddish is that it developed during the migration of Jews to Central Europe from further west and south during the Tenth Century. The language contains elements of Hebrew, French, Italian, and German. After Jews moved even further east in the late Middle Ages, Slavic languages such as Polish, Russian, and Latvian were incorporated. And still later, immigrants to the United States added English elements to Yiddish. (And, as you will read later, Yiddish words became incorporated into colloquial English.)

Maurice Samuel, author and translator of Yiddish literature, wrote in the June 1, 1948, issue of Commentary Magazine:

"Every language has its genius, which is nontransferable; and Yiddish differs from English or French or Italian just as these differ from one another.

"It differs in the same way from German, even though it has taken from a German dialect about eighty-five per cent of its raw material."

It is not the lingua Franca of the Jewish people. Yes, but . . . it was the lingua Franca of the Jews of Eastern Europe. It allowed Jews from different European countries, who may have spoken Russian but not Polish, or Latvian but not French, to converse with each other.

In a parallel development to Yiddish, Jews who lived in countries surrounding the Mediterranean or in the Middle East incorporated similar vernaculars using Spanish or Farsi or

Arabic, and wrote the new hybrid languages in Hebrew letters. A Jew from Yemen would have understood as much Yiddish as did the Amish in *The Frisco Kid*. (Actually, a Yemenite Jew would understand less Yiddish than the Amish - the Amish speak a dialect of German, so they can comprehend Yiddish words that are cognates of German.)

It is not a dead language. Yes, but . . . the number of Yiddish speakers, those who have spoken it from birth, is small. At its peak, before the Holocaust, it was the most widely spoken Jewish language, with an estimated ten to eleven million users; the number now is under two million, and few of them consider Yiddish their primary language.

In my work as a hospice chaplain, I often served elderly patients. Many of them spoke unaccented English, but knew Yiddish, either fluently, having spoken it as a child, or spottily, being comfortable with using Yiddish phrases and expressions. More than once, a family member asked me if I spoke Yiddish because their loved ones, as they descend into dementia, forgot English and spoke only in Yiddish. "Sometimes," one said to me, "my mother doesn't even realize she's speaking in Yiddish, not English." When my grandmother developed Parkinson's disease-related dementia, she eventually could speak only in the Yiddish of her youth, even after having lived in the United States for over fifty years.

In some Orthodox and Chasidic communities in the United States and elsewhere, including Israel, Yiddish is still used for everyday speech, with English (or Hebrew) as a second language. In the United States, the dialectical combination of Yiddish and English spoken by the ultra Orthodox is sometimes referred to rather disparagingly as Yeshivish. The Yiddish words are written in the Latin alphabet and the English ones are spoken with a Yiddish syntax and inflection. The Orthodox community in Israel, however, generally speaks both standard Yiddish and colloquial Hebrew, although the pronunciation is the Ashkenazi of Europe, not the Sephardi of Modern Hebrew; e.g., they say Shabbos, not Shabbat.

Ultra Orthodox Jews in Israel reserve the use of Hebrew for study and prayer, and refuse to speak anything but Yiddish or other secular languages for mundane, everyday communication. The commemorative plaque outside the Jerusalem home of Eliezer ben Yehuda (1858-1922), the "Father of Modern Hebrew" responsible for almost single-handedly reviving Hebrew as a spoken language, is regularly vandalized or removed, presumably by those who believe the use of Hebrew for worldly commerce is a desecration of the *loshn kodesh*, holy language.

From the earliest days of Zionism, debate raged over whether Hebrew or Yiddish should be the language of the Jewish Homeland. (The arguments in favor of Yiddish seemed to have ignored the large population of Sephardim to whom Yiddish was even more foreign than Modern Hebrew.)

In the United States and other Western countries, the successful assimilation of the Eastern European Jewish immigrants meant that the following generations did not know Yiddish. The language was virtually eradicated in Europe by the murder of the majority of its speakers in the Holocaust. Stalin and other leaders of the USSR destroyed much of its remnants.

On the night of August 12-13, 1952, five of the most prominent Yiddish poets living in the Soviet Union were secretly executed in the basement of the Lubyanka Prison in Moscow. Stalin had ordered the executions, claiming the poets, all of whom were associated with the Jewish Anti-Fascist Committee, established by Stalin in 1942 to enlist the aid of the Allied nations' Jewish communities in the Soviet struggle again Hitler, were spies and traitors.

Pronouncements of the death of Yiddish, however, have been premature. Yes, it is an academic discipline that is studied, researched, and taught at the college level. Yes, much of its rich literature is known only in translation, or in "sanitized" Broadway versions. Yet, despite its reputation as a scholarly pursuit or quaint anachronism, it continues to be spoken and, more importantly, to evolve. And to Jews whose ancestors came from Eastern Europe, even for those who speak no Yiddish at all, it still remains the *mame-loshn*, mother tongue.

II. Yiddish Grammar

Although this is not a how-to-speak-Yiddish book, it is important to understand some basic grammatical rules. These are general ones, as it is outside the scope of this book to examine grammatical details, irregular nouns and verbs, and all the other idiosyncrasies of a spoken language.

Unlike English, but like most other languages, the nouns are male, female, and neuter, and the verbs, adjectives, and articles agree with the gender. There are several different plural endings for nouns: -n, -en, -er, -s, -es.

For adjectives, the masculine ending is -er, while the feminine, the neuter, and the plural are all -e.

The definite articles are der (masculine), di (feminine), and dos (neuter) for singular nouns. All plural nouns take the feminine, di. The indefinite article is a, the same as in English.

Yiddish is a Teutonic language, but because of the influence of Slavic languages differs from it in a few ways. Unlike German, for example, the verb in Yiddish generally follows the subject, in the same manner as in English, rather than being at the end of the sentence as in German. There are, of course, exceptions, but most of those have to do with emphasis. (The same is true in conversational English: A polite invitation - "Do you want to go to dinner with me?" - can become one of incredulity - "Me, you want to go to dinner with?")

Like German and English, but unlike some Romance languages such as Italian, the adjective precedes the noun in Yiddish. (Interestingly, in Hebrew, the other language of the Jews, but with a Semitic origin, and one which has nothing to do with Yiddish except the etymology of some words in both languages and the alphabet used, the adjective follows the noun.)

In Yiddish, infinitive verbs take the ending -n or -en. The past participle is formed by adding ge- at the beginning and -n, -en, or -t at the end. The past tense is formed by adding hoben (to have) or zein (to be) before the past participle. In the present tense, verbs are conjugated for person and number by the addition of suffixes: the base word (without the infinitive -n suffix) in the first person; -st in the second person singular; -t in the neuter singular and the second person plural; -n in the first and third person plurals.

One standard feature of Yiddish, which it shares with Greek, Hebrew, and most Romance and Slavic languages, but interestingly not with most Teutonic languages, is the use of double negatives. The expression nit kain (not none) is used frequently.

III. A Note on Transliterations

Yiddish is a Germanic language written in Hebrew characters. As with any transliteration, there are always inaccuracies in trying to describe how a word sounds. But there are also problems because of regional pronunciations. In English, for example, is the word "aunt" to be transliterated as "ant" or "ahnt"? Is the opening diphthong in "either" pronounced as long-e or long-i?

In Yiddish, is kugel, a pudding made from noodles, potato, or matzo, pronounced kiggel (as in Galicia, the part of the Austro-Hungarian Empire that changed its nationality depending on who had won the previous war) or koogel (as in Lithuania)? More than one Galitzianer-Litvak intermarried family has been rent asunder by this debate. (In my home, if I make it, it's koogel; if my husband does, it's kiggel.)

In the case of kugel, there is general agreement that the dish is transliterated into English as kugel, even though it is pronounced differently depending on family tradition and country of origin. Not so with other Yiddish words, however. In the case of unleavened bread, "matzo" is the spelling most commonly seen on supermarket boxes, but "matzah" is occasionally seen. (And when I was growing up in Boston, it was pronounced matzie, regardless of spelling.) And there are as many spellings in English of the winter Holiday of Lights as there are days of the holiday: Hanukkah, Hannukkah, Hanuka, Hannukka, Chanukah, Channukah, Chanuka, Channukka.

Only Hanukkah and Chanukah are considered normative transliterations, but neither one accurately describes the pronunciation of the first letter. The word in Hebrew is neither an aspirated "h" as in "hello," nor is it "ch" as in "China." The guttural sound is most like the German ach, which can be rendered in English as "kh." However, seldom (if ever) will the transliteration Khanukah appear (with or without doubled consonants or final "h") in English. (Linguistically, the letter should be written with a dot under an "h" or a dot over a "k.")

For words in this book, I have generally maintained the transliteration spellings that are considered scholarly, except when those spellings are difficult for English-speaking readers to decipher. For example, I have retained "ch" for familiar words such as tuchus (rear end), l'chaim (to life), and the personal name Chaim, even though they are pronounced with a guttural sound. Another exception is challah, the egg bread used on the Sabbath. (And, like the pronunciation of of matzo, in the Boston of my youth, it was pronounced challie.) Not only is it familiar to English speakers, but to spell it phonetically as khallah would make it look too much like the word for "bride," *kallah*. For other, less familiar words, I did use "ch" for the soft sound, and "kh" for the guttural. For example, the slow-cooking stew, a traditional Sabbath afternoon dish, called *cholent*, is pronounced with the soft "ch" sound, and *brokh*, a curse, has the guttural pronunciation.

In addition, I changed the academic transliterations of Yiddish words that have found their way into English usage. Shmuck (slang for penis, used in English as a derisive term similar to "asshole"), for example, is properly transliterated as shmok, and the above-mentioned tuchus as tokhes. But those words look strange to eyes used to American pronunciations of Yiddish. In the same way, I have used "tz" instead of the preferred "ts" since many words, such as mitzvah, matzo, and blintz are familiar to English-speakers. Also, the "ts" transliteration would make some words look like a common English one; e.g., putz should be properly transliterated as pots.

It is standard to use "k" instead of "ck," and I have done so except when the "ck" is more familiar. For consistency, I have used "sh" throughout the book, even when word processing software accept some Yiddish words when they are spelled "sch," but not "sh." The only exceptions are personal and surnames based on Yiddish words and words like borscht (Russian) and kitsch (German).

Unlike English in which "kn" is prounced as "n" (know; knight, knee, knit), in Yiddish each letter is enunciated. To clarify the pronunciation, I have spelled words like knish as k'nish.

For vowel sounds, I have transliterated long-a as "ai," (*maidl* - young woman); long-i as "ei;" (*bubbe meise* - a fairy tale); long-e as "ie" (*mieskeit* - someone homely), except when a different spelling is familiar to English-speakers.

All of these "rules" have made proofreading a nightmare. To give you an idea of the difficulties, my MS Word spellcheck had a nervous breakdown. Or, more accurately, it went on strike. I had to save each chapter as a separate file in order to be able to check even the English spellings of words.

An additional difficulty - and a personal one - is two-fold. First, I do not have good auditory discrimination and am not sure if what I hear is how a word is spelled. Second, I grew up in Boston, so I know that many words are not spelled the way I pronounce them. Yes, I do say "Pahk the cah in Hahvahd Yahd," and I know it is a nonsense sentence because parking is not allowed in Harvard Yard, but I do know how to spell each word. Yet when it comes to Yiddish, I'm never certain if a syllable ends in "ah" (which I hear and say) or "er." My deficiency in auditory discrimination means I cannot tell if a word should be spelled fahblungit or verblungit. (It's actually *farblonget* - lost, confused - which describes how I felt while working on this book and striving for consistency.)

In other words, do not look for a consistent transliteration scheme.

IV. Yiddish Culture

A. Literature

Until the mid-Nineteenth Century, most Yiddish literature was in the form of folk tales, parables, ethical tales, and legends. The Chasidim in particular used parables to disseminate the teachings of their rebbes, who were a combination of rabbi, spiritual leader, advisor, and teacher.

Some proponents of the *Haskalah* (Enlightenment) wrote their own novels and plays to counteract these Chasidic legends.

Because Hebrew was used only for prayer and religious study in Eastern Europe, women, who were not required to pray three times a day or engage in religious study, generally knew only enough Hebrew to be able to say the blessings connected with the home and with ritual purity. They had their own holy book, however, called *Tzena U'rena* ("Come Out and Look," the title a quote from Song of Songs 3:11), which contained Yiddish translations of the weekly Torah and Haftarah portion, plus Yiddish commentaries, stories, and parables based on them.

Zikhroynes Glikl Hameln (The Memoirs of Gluckl of Hamlin) is generally considered to be the first full-length Yiddish book. Born in 1646 in Hamburg, Gluckl married a businessman, and, while helping him run his business, raised twelve children. After he left her a widow at age forty-three, she took complete control of his business, and traveled extensively through Central Europe. The diaries, which were left to her children after her death in 1724 in Metz, provide a detailed look at Jewish life in Central Europe during the late Eighteenth Century. They were not published until 1892.

Dos Klaine Mentshele (The Little Person), published in 1864, is generally considered the first modern Yiddish book. It was written by Sholem Yankev Abramovitsh (1835-1917), who became known as Mendele Moykher Sforim

("Mendel the Book Peddler"), the fictional narrator of many of his stories. He, along with Sholem Rabinovitsh (better known by his penname, Sholem Aleichem) and I. L. Peretz (1852-1915), formed the trio that epitomized Yiddish literature. They are collectively known as *di klasiker* (the classics).

Of the three klasiker, Sholem Aleichem (1859-1916) is the best known to English speakers because of the popularity of the adaptation of his series of short stories, called collectively *Tevye and His Daughters*. The original story is much darker and more tragic than the Broadway or Hollywood musical versions titled *Fiddler on the Roof*.

In the original stories, Shprintze, one of Tevye's seven daughters (there are five in *Fiddler on the Roof*) falls in love with a rich young man, whose uncle thinks she is after his money. He will not allow the marriage, the young man leaves, and Shprintze throws herself into the river and drowns. Tevye's son-in-law Motl becomes ill and suddenly dies. Tevye's wife Golde dies of natural causes. Chava's non-Jewish husband, rather than casting his fate with the Jews, beats Chava, who leaves him and is accepted back into the family.

The name Sholem Aleichem is taken from the phrase used when two Jews greet each other. It means "peace upon you," and the proper response is *aleikhem sholem*, "upon you peace."

The writing gene passed on through the generations, as Bel Kaufman, author of *Up the*

Down Staircase, was Sholem Aleichem's granddaughter.

The most prolific years of Yiddish literature were 1900-1940, but it continues to this day. Isaac Bashevis Singer (1901-1992), is one of the best known of the more modern Yiddish writers, in part because of the movie adaptation of his short story *Yentl der Yeshiva Bokher*, "Yentl, the Yeshiva Boy."

Similar to the "sanitizing" that took place when Sholem Aleichem's stories about Tevye the Dairyman were transformed into *Fiddler on the Roof*, Singer's original short story is more explicitly sexual than Barbra Streisand's movie version. In both a 1975 English-language stage adaptation written by Singer and Leah Napolin and in the original on which it is based, Yentl tells her study partner, who discovers her real sex, that she is "neither one sex nor the other" and has "the soul of a man in the body of a woman." Many in the gay, lesbian, bisexual, and transgender community take this statement to mean that Yentl was not a proto-feminist (the implication of the movie), but a transgender, in part because at the end of the story, Yentl decides to continue to live her life as her male alter ego.

In 1978, Isaac Bashevis Singer won the Nobel Prize for Literature, the only Yiddish writer to have done so, not only assuring his legacy but that of Yiddish literature in general.

B. Newspapers

An example of the decline - or evolution, perhaps - of the everyday use of Yiddish can be seen by looking at the history of Jewish newspapers, particularly the *Forvertz*. A daily Yiddish-language socialist-leaning newspaper, the *Forvertz* was the main source of news, gossip, advice, literature, culture, and entertainment for new immigrants and their children.

From 1885 to 1914, over one hundred fifty Yiddish publications - dailies, weeklies, monthlies, quarterlies - were established in New York City alone. Twenty of these New York publications were daily newspapers, with as many as six competing with each other at a time. During the year 1915-16, there were five dailies in New York City with a circulation of five hundred thousand readers. Abraham Cahan, the founder and editor of the *Forvertz* until his death in 1950, wrote, "The five million Jews living under the czar had not a single Yiddish daily paper even when the government allowed such publication, while [we] in America publish six dailies, [plus] countless Yiddish weeklies and monthlies. . . . New York [is] the largest Yiddish book market in the world."

When the *Forvertz* published its first issue on April 22, 1897, there were thirteen Yiddish newspapers in the United States. Within twenty years, it had become the largest of them, with a circulation of two hundred seventy-five thousand. In addition, it had twelve metropolitan editions in cities from Boston to Los Angeles, with a readership of another quarter of a million.

Circulation began to decline after the passage of restrictive immigration quotas in 1923, and continued to fall. Almost a century after its founding, it became a weekly in 1983 and added a supplement in English. Seven years after that adaptation, it evolved into an English-language weekly, the *Forward*, and published a separate biweekly supplement in Yiddish. The English weekly's circulation peaked at around 26,000 and the Yiddish edition's at around 3,000. In 2017, it changed formats again, becoming a monthly magazine in print, and expanding its news coverage online. The mission of the *Forvertz* was to Americanize the new Jewish immigrants. The decline in circulation in a sense was a testament to its success.

The *Forward* published *tzeitung romans* (literally, "newspaper novels," referring to novels serialized in newspapers, such as Charles Dickens' works when they were first published), but in the Twenty-First Century they were written in the English of Anne Roiphe, not in the Yiddish of Isaac Bashevis Singer.

Other Yiddish newspapers often ran stories they either made up themselves (a la Hearst) or cribbed from the general circulation press. The *Philadelphia Yiddish Weekly* once misinterpreted the headline in the shipping page of an English language paper that read "The Empress of China Arrived Yesterday on Her Maiden Voyage." The editor, Hayim Malitz, thought the headline meant that China's unmarried queen had come to Philadelphia to find a husband, and ran a story to that effect.

The most famous of the features in the *Forvertz* was *A Bintel Brief*, literally, "a bundle of letters," an advice column that set the model for all the advice columnists to follow. Abraham Cahan answered questions that reflected the new immigrants' bewilderment at American mores and customs. The concerns addressed covered all aspects of life, from unemployment to marital problems to conflicts with children who rejected the Old World customs of their parents. Today, the Bintel Brief continues - as "The Bintel Blog."

Another interesting feature the *Forvertz* ran was called *A Gallarya fon Farshvondne Manner*, translated as "A Gallery of Disappeared Husbands." Often, the men would emigrate first, in order to earn money and become established before sending tickets for their wives and children to follow. Sometimes, they came to enjoy the freedoms of being a bachelor in this new world too much, and did not want to go back to the restrictions of married life. Their wives would list their names in the *Forvertz*, along with their pictures, to embarrass them into fulfilling their familial responsibilities. The movie *Hester Street* is an excellent portrayal of the cultural clash between the Americanized husband and the Old World wife who joins him later in New York.

C. Theater

Not surprisingly, Yiddish theater flourished during the same period as Yiddish literature. All the various genres of plays were represented, from broad farce to melodrama, from musical revues to experimental theater, from Yiddish translations of Shakespeare (*King Lear* and *Hamlet* were particularly popular) to political satire.

Yiddish theaters existed in every large (and some not-so-large) community where there were Jews. Following the 1881 assassination of Tzar Alexander II, whose reign had been marked by the relaxation of many harsh laws against the Jews, there was a backlash against his pro-Semitic rulings, and by 1883, Yiddish theaters were banned in Imperial Russia. The ban was not lifted until 1904, by which time Yiddish theater had moved to Western Europe and to the United States, where it grew and prospered. Just before World War I, there were twenty-two Yiddish theaters and two Yiddish vaudeville houses in New York City, and over two hundred Yiddish theaters were established throughout the United States between 1890 and 1940.

The Holocaust brought an end to Yiddish theater in Europe, and assimilation and the ascendency of Hebrew curtailed its popularity elsewhere. Today, the State Jewish Theater of Bucharest, Romania, considered the birthplace of Yiddish theater (Abraham Goldfaden established the first professional Yiddish acting troupe there in 1876), still produces some Yiddish plays, but with simultaneous Romanian translation. In Israel, the Yiddishpiel Theatre Company, which was founded in 1987, presents new Yiddish plays. In North America, the Dora Wasserman Yiddish Theatre of Montreal, established in 1958, and the Folksbiene (People's Stage) Yiddish Theatre of New York, founded in 1915, are still producing Yiddish plays.

D. Film

Yiddish films are not as numerous as theatrical plays were. In the years between the two World Wars, approximately one hundred Yiddish films were produced. Four of them, made in Poland by Joseph Green, have become classics, especially the two which starred Molly Picon: *Yidl Mitn Fidl* (The Little Jew with a Fiddle, 1936), in which she plays a young woman who disguises herself as a man so she can join a band of traveling musicians; and *Mamele* (The Little Mother, 1938) in which she is responsible for raising her brothers and sisters after the death of her mother. Both are musical comedies. The other two Green films are *Der Purimspiler* (The Jester, 1937), a romantic comedy, and *A Brivele der Mamen* (A Letter to Mama, 1938), a sentimental melodrama.

Many of the Yiddish films were adaptations of Yiddish literary works, such as *The Dybbuk*, but many others were melodramas, comedies, or musicals. *Shund* (trash) was as popular a genre for movies as it was for plays.

Yiddish film did not survive either the Holocaust or the decline of Yiddish as a spoken language. In a 1991 documentary, Green, then ninety-one years old, said, "Six million of my best customers perished."

E. Actors

Many veterans of the Yiddish theater made successful transitions to the English-language stage (and film and TV). One of the giants of Yiddish theater Jacob Adler, known as the "Great Eagle" (*Adler* is German for eagle), began his career in Russia, gained fame in London, and was idolized in the United States. In 1903, his fame reached international superstar status after he received rave reviews as Shylock in the Broadway production of *The Merchant of Venice*.

Jacob Adler's daughter Stella was the only American actor to have been trained by Stanislavski in what became known as Method Acting. She founded an acting school that still bears her name (and reputation). His brother, Luther Adler, also gained fame in English-language plays and films after being in the Yiddish theater.

Another great of the Yiddish theater, Boris Tomashevsky, did not make the transition to the English-language stage. Unlike Adler, who preferred serious dramas, Tomashevsky starred in what was disparagingly referred to as *shund* (trash) plays - melodramas, farces, and other light works. Tomashevsky's grandson is the renowned conductor Michael Tilson-Thomas.

From the 2005 musical adaptation of *The Producers*:

Max: I was a protege of the great Boris Tomashevsky. He taught me everything I know. I'll never forget, he turned to me on his death bed and said: "*Maxella, alle menschen muss zu machen, jeden tug a gentzen kak'n!*"

Nun: What does that mean?

Max: Who knows? I don't speak Yiddish. Strangely enough, neither did he.

[The phrase means, "Little Max, everyone has to take a crap every day."]

Many Yiddish actors did make the crossover from Yiddish theater to English-language productions. They include:

Reizl Bozyk, mainly a Yiddish actor, was the Bubbe in *Hester Street*.

Joseph Buloff, had roles in many television shows as well as movies. One of his last roles, only two years before his death in 1985 at age eighty-six, was in the movie *Reds*.

Fyvush Finkel had several roles in television and films before becoming beloved as a regular on the television series *Picket Fences*.

Leo Fuchs, whose mother was a star of the Yiddish theater, was a character actor who was nicknamed "The Yiddish Fred Astaire." Among other roles, he was the Chief Rabbi in *The Frisco Kid*.

Estelle Getty, "Sophia" on The Golden Girls, got her start in the Yiddish theater and in the Borscht Belt.

Sam Jafe, who, despite his numerous roles, will always be known as Dr. Zorba in Ben Casey, began in Yiddish theater.

Sidney Lumet, best known as a director, made his stage debut at age four in the Yiddish Art Theater in New York.

Walter Matthau, who, despite looking like a sad bloodhound, always managed to woo and win the likes of Sophia Loren and Goldie Hawn, got his start in the Yiddish theater at age eleven.

Paul Muni, one of only six actors to receive an Oscar nomination as Best Actor in a Lead Role for his first movie (in *The Valiant*, 1929), was nominated five more times and won for *The Story of Louis Pasteur*, in 1935.

Leonard Nimoy, forever known as Mr. Spock from the *Star Trek* franchise, worked in a Yiddish theater group when he first moved to Los Angeles.

David Opatoshu, after years as a character actor, won an Emmy in 1990 for Outstanding Guest Actor in a Drama Series for his role in *Gabriel's Fire*.

Molly Picon, who at the age of eighty-six acted in *Cannonball Run II*, was a star not only of the Yiddish theater but of Yiddish films.

Menasha Skulnik, a luminary of the Yiddish theater, won a Tony for Best Actor in a Musical for his performance in the Broadway play *The Zulu and the Zayda*, in 1964.

Harold J. Stone, a character actor who had supporting roles in numerous films and television shows, started on the stage as a child with his father, a Yiddish actor.

F. Music

Much Jewish music was either liturgical (many of the great Jewish opera singers were trained as cantors - and vice versa) or instrumental. The only musical genres that can be called "Yiddish" are folksongs, lullabies, show tunes, and popular songs with Yiddish lyrics. Klezmer, a type of music played at weddings and other celebrations, is often called "Yiddish," but is more properly described as Eastern European Jewish because it is mainly instrumental.

The word *klezmer*, from the Hebrew *klai zemer*, (vessels of song, musical instruments), refers to Eastern European Jewish itinerant musicians and to their musical instruments. *Klezmorim* (the plural form of the word) were looked down upon by the religious because of their secular way of life. They often traveled with the Romany, and there are influences of each musical form in the other's music.

Klezmer music has been compared to Dixieland and has been called "Jewish jazz." With its reliance on instruments like the clarinet, it also influenced modern composers, including Aaron Copeland, Leonard Bernstein, and George Gershwin (particularly the opening bars of

Rhapsody in Blue), as well as Big Band clarinetist Benny Goodman.

The mid-to-late Twentieth Century saw a "klez revival." Unlike traditional *klezmer* music, the contemporary groups include singing, and many of the songs have English lyrics. In 2006, the Klezmatics, one of the most popular bands of the klez revival, recorded *Woody Guthrie's Happy Joyous Hannukah*, which set Guthrie's words to *klezmer* music. That same year, they won the Grammy for Contemporary World Music for their album *Wonder Wheel*, in which they set lyrics written by Guthrie when he lived in the Coney Island section of Brooklyn to various musical genres, including *klezmer*.

Chapter One

A Brokh tzu Dein Lebn!
Curses and Curse Words

It may seem as though it should be easy to "talk dirty" in a language with over sixty vulgarisms, but ask many Yiddish speakers and they will say they do not know any curse words. (There is a gender division here: the women don't know any - or won't admit they do - while the men say they know quite a few.) No one, however, will deny that Yiddish is replete with wonderful curses.

A curse is not the same as a curse word. I was looking for a book on Yiddish curses that I knew we owned, and could not find it on our bookshelves. I finally found it in my then thirteen-year-old son's room, under his bed. He had thought he would be able to learn from its pages how to say the "S-word" without being reprimanded. Much to his disappointment, the book contains lists of curses, not curse words.

A curse word is an expletive; it is the expression you use when you hit your thumb with a hammer and yell, "Fuck!" A curse is a hex. It is when you wish someone ill, as in the oft quoted "May you grow like an onion, with your head in the ground and your ass in the air."

In Yiddish, cursing, in the sense of casting a spell, is a time-honored tradition. Entire books have been devoted to lists of curses, covering all types of situations. If you have daughters, "They should be like the flowers of the field - wither and fade away." If you have sons, "They should be so smart that they learn the Mourner's Prayer before their Bar Mitzvah portions" (i.e., you should die before they turn thirteen). If your health is good, "You should outlive everyone but your mother-in-law." (Mother-in-law jokes, it seems, are universal.) If you are wealthy, "All your competitors' stores should burn down except yours, and yours should burn down the day the insurance lapses."

Some curses can be quite vulgar. For example, you would not hear "You should crap glass and piss vinegar" in polite company. But most Yiddish curses are in the category of humorous, although mean-spirited, wishes. Especially clever are the ones that start out sounding like a blessing: "Your chickens should lay many eggs each day...in your neighbor's yard;" "You should never develop stomach trouble...from too rich a diet;" "You should have many descendants...and have to support them all;" "God should answer all your prayers...and then mistake your worst enemy for you."

Yiddish curses are often translated into English translations using the phrase "may you," but that is much more polite than the literal Yiddish. In Yiddish, curses generally begin with or include the word *zol*, which means "should." The formulation is seen as *zol er* (he should), *zol zi* (she should), *zol es* (it should), *zoln* (they should), or, if you are confronting your antagonist in person, *zolst* (you should), as in the universal

50

parental lament, "You should only have children like you so you should know what it is like."

A curse in English such as "Go to Hell" (which has a Yiddish equivalent: *Gai in drerd arein*) pales beside a curse in Yiddish like "Your enemies should get cramps in their legs from dancing on your grave." Who needs curse words when you have such inventive curses instead?

During the 2016 Presidential campaign, a list of "Yiddish Curses for Republican Jews" went viral on Facebook and elsewhere online. It had already been in existence for about four years. The earliest reference I could find was in an article in the August 30, 2012, issue of the *New Yorker*, by Michael Schulman about a project launched by his friends Ben Abramowitz and Rachel Shukert.
(http://www.newyorker.com/humor/daily-shouts/yiddish-curses-for-republican-jews)

The next online version I found was on the blogsite "*Ma Hamatzav* (Waz up?)," by Rabbi Aaron Spiegel; it was later reprinted in the December 12, 2016, issue of *Jewish Currents*.
(http://jewishcurrents.org/yiddish-curses-for-republican-jews/).

Several other edited and revised versions began circulating in 2016, most incorporating the original lists, but with some differences. There is also a Facebook page. Below is as complete and accurate a listing of unique curses as I could compile. Apologies if I omitted one of your favorites.

May you sell everything and retire to Florida just as global warming makes it uninhabitable.

May you live to a hundred and twenty without Social Security or Medicare.

May you live to a hundred and twenty on your Social Security vouchers.

May you make a fortune, and lose it all in one of Sheldon Adelson's casinos.

May you live to a ripe old age, and may the only people who come visit you be Mormon missionaries.

May your grandchildren baptize you after you're dead.

May your son be elected President, and may you have no idea what you did with his goddamn birth certificate.

May your insurance company decide constipation is a pre-existing condition.

May your insurance company decide lactose intolerance is a pre-existing condition.

May you feast every day on chopped liver with onions, chicken soup with dumplings, baked carp with horseradish, braised meat with vegetable stew, latkes, and may every bite of it be contaminated with E. Coli, because the government gutted the E.P.A.

May you find yourself insisting to a roomful of skeptics that your great-grandmother was "legitimately" raped by Cossacks.

May you have a rare disease and need an operation that only one surgeon in the world, the winner of the Nobel Prize for Medicine, is able to perform. And may he be unable to perform it because he doesn't take your insurance. And may that Nobel Laureate be your son.

May the state of Arizona expand their definition of "suspected illegal immigrants" to "anyone who doesn't hunt."

May you be reunited in the world to come with your ancestors, who were all socialist garment workers.

May your child give his Bar Mitzvah speech on the genius of Karl Marx.

May the synagogue raise your required donation to the building fund in proportion to your tax cut.

May you find yourself explaining to El Al security how you forgot to bring the permit for your concealed hand gun.

May your daughter become engaged to a wealthy, brilliant, Jewish man, and may the Romney sticker on the back of your car get you blackballed by every wedding planner, hairdresser, makeup artist, dress designer, and florist in town.

Here is a sampling of creative Yiddish imprecations. There are more scattered throughout other chapters of the book.

A fei'er zol im trefn! - He should meet a fire! [He should burn up!]

A kholaire ahf dir! - A cholera on you!

A meshuganer zol men oyshraibn, un im arainshraibn. - They should free a madman, and lock him up instead.

A mise meshune ahf dir! - An unnatural death on you!

53

A shvartz yor ahf dir! - A difficult year on you!

Azoy fil ritzinoyl zol er oystrink'n. - He should drink too much castor oil.

Brenen - To burn.

Brenen zol er! - He should burn (in hell)!

Brenen zolstu afn fei'er! - You should burn in fire!

Zol er brenem in gehenem. - He should burn in Hell.

Brokh - Curse

A brokh! - Oh hell! Damn it!

A brokh iz mir! - I am cursed!

A brokh tzu dein lebn! - A curse on your life!

A brokh tzu dein lebn, nish far dir degakht! - A curse on your life, may it never happen to you!

A brokh tzu dir! - A curse on you!

Er zol kak'n mit blit un mit aiter. - He should crap blood and pus.

Es iz nit geshtoygen un nit gefloygen! - It never rose and it never flew! (The English version would be: They ran it up the flag pole and no one saluted; i.e., it was a bullshit idea.)

Farshporn zol er oyf shtain? - Why should he bother to get up?

Finstere laid zol nor di mama oyf im zen. - Black sorrow is all that his mother should see of him.

Gai - Go!

Gai avek! Go away!

Gai in drerd arein! - Go to hell!

Gai plotz! - Go blow up!

54

Gai shoyn, gai! - Go away already!

Gai strashe di vantzn! - Go threaten the bedbugs (i.e., you don't scare me!).

Heng dikh oyf a tzikershtrikl vestu hobn a zisn toyt. - Hang yourself with a sugar rope and you'll have a sweet death. (Similar to "hoisted on his own petard.")

Hindert heizer zol er hobn, in yeder hoyz a hindert tzimern, in yeder tzimer tzvonsik betn un kadukhes zol im varfn fin ain bet in der tzvaiter. - A hundred houses he should have, in every house a hundred rooms and in every room twenty beds, and a delirious fever should drive him from bed to bed.

Ikh faif ahf dir! - I whistle on you! (In colloquial English, I wash my hands of you.)

Ikh hob - I'll have

Ikh hob dikh in bod! - I'll have you in the bath! (Watch your back. I'll get you when you least expect it.)

Ikh hob dikh in drerd! - I'll have you in hell. (To hell with you!)

Ikh hob dir! - I'll have you! (I know what you're up to. Drop dead!)

Ikh hob im in bod! - I'll have him in the bath!

Ikh hob im in drerd! - I'll have him in hell. (To hell with him!)

In di zumerdike teg zol er zitzn shive, un in di vinterdike nekht zikh reisn ahf di tzain. - On summer days he should mourn, and on wintry nights, he should torture himself.

Khasene hobn zol er mit di malekh hamoves tokhter. - He should marry the daughter of the Angel of Death.

Lakhn zol er mit yashtherkes. - He should laugh with lizards. (Lizards aren't known for laughing, so he should never laugh or be happy again.)

Lig in drerd! - Lay in the ground! Bury yourself! Get lost! Drop dead!

Loz mikh tzu ruh! - Leave me in peace; leave me alone!

Makeh - Plague, disease

A makeh ahf dir! - A plague on you!

A makeh in yenems oren iz nit shver tzu trogen. - Another's disease isn't hard to endure.

A mol iz der refueh erger fon der makeh. - Sometimes the cure is worse than the disease.

Er zol hobn paroys makehs bashotn mit oybes kretz. - He should have Pharaoh's plagues sprinkled with Job's scabies.

Got zol oyf im onshik'n fin di tzen makehs di beste. - God should visit upon him the best of the Ten Plagues.

Migulgl zol er vern in a hengleihter, by tog zol er hengen, un bei nakht zol er brenen. - He should be transformed into a chandelier; by day he should hang, and by night he should burn.

Nem zikh a vane! - Take a bath! (Go jump in the lake!)

Oyf doktoyrim zol er dos avekgebn. - He should give it (his money) all away to doctors.

Oyskrenk'n zol er dus mame's milakh. - He should get so sick as to cough up his mother's milk.

Shtainer zol zi hobn, nit kain kinder. - Stones she should have, and not children.

Trink'n zoln im piavkes. - Leeches should drink him dry.

Vi tzu derleb ikh im shoyn tzu bagrobn. - I should outlive him long enough to bury him.

Zai nit kain Veizoso! - Don't be Veizoso (one of Haman's sons)! Don't be a fool! Don't be a shmuck!

Zein mazl zol im leihtn vi di levone in sof khoydesh. - His luck should be as bright as a new moon.

Zol er krenken un gedenken. - He should suffer and remember.

Zol er lebn - oder nit lang. - He should live - but not long.

Zol er vern dershtikt. - He should be strangled.

Zol er vern gesharget. - He should be murdered.

Zol es im onkumn vos ikh vintsh im, khotsh a helft, khotsh halb, khotsh a tzent khailik. - What I wish on him should come true, most, even half, even just ten percent.

Zolst habn a ziser toyt - a vagon mit tzuker zol dir iberforn. - You should have a sweet death - a wagon full of sugar should run you over.

Zolst habn a zun vos men ruft nokh dir - un in gikhn. - You should have a son named for you -

and soon. (Ashkenazi Jews name their children after someone who is deceased.)

Chapter Two

A Shprikhvort Iz a Vorvort
A Proverb Is a True Word

Wherever spoken language existed, so did proverbs, aphorisms, maxims, and words of wisdom. Not only are they known in every language and society throughout the world, but they are considered a vibrant part of those cultures' folklore. Proverbs were already an ancient oral tradition when King Solomon began collecting them in the second half of the Tenth Century BCE. The earliest ones have been traced to Twenty-Sixth Century BCE Egypt, and Aristotle considered them the remnants of an older philosophy.

Yiddish has thousands of proverbs and sayings. Pithy, humorous, wise, with a central kernel of truth, many Yiddish proverbs are translated from Polish, Russian, or other languages familiar to Jews living in those countries. Many sayings and proverbs are scattered throughout this book. Below is just a small sampling of others. Some are familiar words of wisdom to English speakers; others should be. They all fit the definition of a proverb: a concise phrase that encapsulates a universal truth.

A falsheh matba'ieh farliert men nit. - A bad penny always turns up.

Proverbs sometimes contradict each other. In English we have both, "Distance makes the

59

heart grow fonder," and "Out of sight, out of mind." In Yiddish, there's *A freint bekamt men umzist; a soyneh muz men zikh koyfn.* (A friend you get for nothing; an enemy has to be bought.), and *A freint darf men zikh koyfn; sonem krigt men umzist.* (A friend you have to buy; enemies you get for nothing.)

A guten vet der shaink vit kalyeh makh, un a shlekhtne vet der bes-hamedresh nit fairkhtn. - A good person won't be made bad by a tavern, and a bad one won't be reformed by the synagogue.

A gutter feint iz oft besser fon a bruder. - A good friend is often better than a brother.

A katz meg oykh kuk'n oyfen kaisser. - A cat can look at a king.

A ligner dark hoben a guten zekhron. - A liar needs a good memory.

A ligner hert zikh zeine ligen azoy lang ein biz er glaibt zikh alain. - A liar tells his story so often even he believes it.

A nar bleibt a nar. - A fool remains a fool.

A nar farlirt un a kluger gefint. - A fool loses and a clever man finds.

A nar gait in bod arein un fargest zikh dos ponim optzuvashn. - A fool goes to the baths and forgets to wash his face.

A nar gait tzvai mol dort, vu a kluger gait nit kain aintzik mol. - A fool goes there [makes a bad decision] twice, while a clever man doesn't go even once.

A nar git, a kluger nemt. - A fool gives [advice], a wise man takes.

A nar ken a mol zogen a gleikh vort. - Even a fool can sometimes say something clever.

A shlekhte sholem iz besser vi a gutter krig. - A bad peace is better than a good war.

Aider men zogt aroys s'vort, iz men a har; dernokh iz men a nar. - Before you say a word you're a master; afterwards, you're a fool.

Arumik zikh mit dvarfs tut nisht makhn ir a riz. - Surrounding yourself with dwarfs does not make you a giant.

Az di bubbe volt gehat baitzim volt zi gevain mein zaide. - If my grandmother had balls, she'd be my grandfather.

Az dos hartz iz ful, gai'en di oygen iber. - When the heart is full, the eyes overflow.

Az meshiakh vet kumen, vellen alleh krankeh oysgehailt verren; nor a nar vet bleiben a nar. - When the Messiah comes, all the sick will be healed; only a fool will stay a fool.

Az ikh vel zein vi yener, ver vet zein vi ikh? - If I would be like someone else, who would be like me?

Az men ken nit iberharn dos shlekhteh, ken men dos guteh nit derleben. - If you can't endure the bad, you won't live to witness the good.

Az men muz, ken men. - When one must, one can. [Necessity is the mother of invention.]

Az se brent, iz a fei'er. - Where there's smoke, there's fire.

On the back cover of Fred Kogos' *From Shmear to Eternity* is a variation on this famous proverb: *Az sie brent, es a lox.* - Where there's smoke, there's lox.

Besser tzu shtarben shtai'endik aider tzu leben oyf di k'ni. - Better to die upright than to live on your knees.

During the Holocaust, many Jews either joined with other partisan groups fighting against the Nazis or formed their own underground resistance groups. Their rallying cry was a song written by Hirsh Blik, with music by Dmitri Pokrass, called *Zog Nit Keyn Mol Az Du Gaist Dem Letzten Veg*, "Never Say That You Are Going Your Last Way." All Holocaust Memorial Day commemorations include, in Yiddish and English, the singing of The Song of the Partisans.

Der mentsh trakht, un Got lakht. - A man thinks and God laughs. [Man supposes and God disposes.]

Der vos hot nit fazukht bitterreh, vaist nit voz zies iz. - One who has never tasted the bitter cannot know the sweet.

Der vos shveigt maint oykh epes. - He who is silent still means something.

Di epeleh falt nit veit fon baimeleh. - The apple doesn't fall far from the tree.

Di grub iz shoyn ofen un der mentsh tut nokh hofen. - The grave is already open and man still hopes.

Di länger ein Blinder lebt, desto mehr sieht er. - The longer a blind man lives, the more he sees.

Faren dokter un aren beder zeinen nit kain soydes. - There are no secrets from a doctor or a bathhouse attendant.

Fon ain oks tzit men akin tzvai fellen nit arop. - You can't get two skins from one ox. (There is a variation: You can't sit on two chairs with one tuchus.)

Fon dein moyl in Gotz oyeren. - From your mouth to God's ears

Fon kin'ah vert sin'ah. - Envy breeds hate.

Got hat eine Welt voller kleiner Weltchen ershaffen. - God created one world full of small worlds.

Nit dos iz shain, vos iz shain, nor dos, vos es gefelt. - Beautiful is not what is beautiful, but what one likes. [Beauty is in the eye of the beholder.]

Nit kain entfer iz oykh an entfler. - No answer is also an answer

Oder es helft nit oder men darf es nit. - Either it doesn't help or you don't need it.

Oyf vemens vogen me zitzt, zingt men dem lied. - On whoever's wagon you're sitting, that's whose tune you're singing.

Reden iz shver un shveigen kenmen nit. - Speech is difficult, but silence impossible.

Reden iz zilber, shveigen iz gold. - Speech is silver, silence is golden.

Shainkeit fargait, khokhme bashtait. - Beauty fades, wisdom stays

Ven me lakht ze'en alleh; ven me vaint zet kainer nisht. - When you laugh, all see; when you cry, no one sees.

Ven men darf hoben moy'akh, helft nit kain koy'akh. - When you need brains, brawn won't help.

Ven si farleshen zikh di likht, haiben on tasntzen di meiz. - When the lights go out, the mice dance. [When the cat's away, the mice will play.]

Ver filt zikh, der meynt zikh. - Who feels guilty, feels responsible.

Vos mer gevart, mer genart. - He who hesitates is lost.

Yeder hartz hot soydes. - Every heart has secrets.

Yeder mentsh iz oyf zikh alain blind. - Every man is blind to his own faults.

Chapter Three

Bei Mir Bist Du Shoen
It's All Yinglish to Me

In many ways, this book is about how to speak Yinglish, not Yiddish. Leo Rosten, author of *The Joys of Yiddish*, is credited with coining the word Yinglish to refer to an amalgam of English and Yiddish, a hybrid of English words given a Yiddish inflection, or Yiddish words given new meanings. Many native English speakers, including non-Jews, use Yinglish without being aware of it. Yinglish words can be heard daily, in common speech and in the mass media. The words have become so engrained into the English vernacular that, even though some may sound Yiddish, they are as much a part of Standard English as any slang.

In addition, there are several words that Rosten dubbed Ameridish, meaning they were used only in the United States. Many Yiddish language writers think Yinglish and Ameridish are synonymous because of the universal prevalence of U.S. television shows, not to mention the Internet. Some words listed below, however, are used only in the United States and others only in Great Britain.

There is also a third hybrid of Yiddish and English, specific to certain Orthodox communities, dubbed Yeshivish. It is characterized by vocabulary, syntax, and inflections that combine both Yiddish and

English. It is used by native English speakers who have picked up the "dialect" in the Jewish schools they attend. It differs from Yiddish in that the words are written in English characters, not Hebrew, and the Yiddish words are conjugated as though they were in English. The speech sounds like slightly eccentric or idiomatic Standard English.

Listed below are just a few of the more colorful and familiar Yinglish words:

Fin

Five-dollar bill, from Yiddish *funf,* five

I had to pay a fin to park for a quarter of an hour!

Futz

To fool around with, to mess with; has added advantage for teenagers of sounding like an expletive deleted. Its etymology is probably the Yiddish *arumfortzen*, to fart around.

Stop futzing around with the remote and find something to watch already.

Gazump

To cheat someone out of a property by bidding more than the previously accepted offer. The word is used in Britain and Australia to refer to a house purchase.

I had agreed to buy their house, but before we had signed the contract, my roommate gezumped me.

Originally, the word gazump meant to swindle, which lends credence to the theory that the word comes from the Yiddish *gezumf*, to cheat or overcharge.

Gunsel

In common usage, a hoodlum, armed gangster.

That bully down the street walks around with a Super Soaker and pretends he's a gunsel.

Although the word gunsel is usually used to refer to a gunman, it originally meant a young homosexual hobo who was partners with an older tramp. It comes from the Yiddish gentzl, little goose. In The Maltese Falcon, when Sam Spade refers to Wilmer Cook as a gunsel, he is speaking of his sexual orientation and relationship with Kaspar Gutman, not his handgun. Dashiell Hammett managed to sneak the word past the censor, who thought it meant a hoodlum.

Ishkabbible

A dismissive statement. "Who cares?"

They're announcing the Grammy nominees today? *Ishkabbible.*

The word *Ishkabbible* first appeared in a 1913 song, lyrics written by Sam M Lewis and music by George W Meyer, called *Isch Gabibble* (I Should Worry). The actor Merwyn Bogue used the song in his act and took the stage name Ish Kabibble. The phrase has widely been considered to be Yiddish in origin, although there is no concensus as to its etymology. There are many linguists, however, who dismiss its connection to Yiddish, as the word bibble, a cognate of "babble," appeared as early as the Sixteenth Century in Shakespeare's Twelfth Night: "Endeavour thy selfe to sleepe, and leave thy vain bibble babble."

Jalopy

An old, broken down car.

My son wants a new car, but I'd rather he drive a jalopy so we don't have to pay as much insurance.

It is possible the word jalopy comes from the Yiddish (which borrowed it from Polish) *shlappe*, an old horse. A more likely explanation is that the word comes from Jalapa, Mexico, where many used cars wound up.

Kibosh

To put the kibosh on something means to cancel it out, to dismiss it. It most likely comes from Yiddish, and the most plausible explanation is it comes from the Yiddish word *kabbastn*, to suppress.

My twelve year old wanted to go to an R-rated movie, but I put the kibosh on his plans.

Kokhalein

Literally, cook alone; figuratively a summer cottage with a kitchen, a bungalow. It comes from two Yiddish words *kokhn*, to cook, and *alein*, alone.

Every summer, my grandparents would get away from the hot city and stay at a *kokhalein* in the Catskills.

The 1999 movie A Walk on the Moon shows what a *kokhalein* resort was like.

Mazoola

Money. The word comes from the Yiddish *mezumen*, cash.

By the time she was thirteen, my daughter preferred to stay home instead of going to camp so she could babysit and earn some mazoola.

Ootz

Pester; tease or tweak; sometimes spelled "utz," but the word has nothing to do with a Pennsylvania Dutch brand of potato chips.

If you *ootz* the cat, she'll scratch you.

If we just *ootz* the proposal a bit more, we should be ready to send it out.

Shmegegge

Buffoon, idiot

Do you know what that *shmegge* did? He went to an Eagles game in below freezing weather, and took off his shirt to show off his green chest.

Shmo

A nobody, a jerk

He's not important, just a Joe Shmo.

Many Yiddishists believe the cartoonist Al Capp named his character the schmoo after the

Yiddish word *shmo*. It was a formless blob that would transform itself into any kind of food people wanted.

Shnook
An ineffectual, dorky type. Someone you can't take seriously.

I wouldn't hire him as a representative of the company. He's a nice guy, but such a shnook that he'd lose us clients.

Shamus
A detective, comes from *shames*, a watchman.

I always liked Bogart better as a shamus than a criminal.

Shemozzle
British slang for a quarrel, brawl, confusing situation or unfortunate plight, the word probably comes from *shlimazel*. The word is used in Ireland during the game of hurling (not to be confused with what fraternity brothers often do on Saturday nights).

Did you see the news last night about the *shemozzle* outside the pub?

My credit card payment got lost in the mail. What a *shemozzle*!

Spiel
Glib talk, patter, sometimes transliterated as shpeel, from the Yiddish word for play, but usually spelled in English using the German

spelling. Spiel can be a verb, as in playing an instrument, or a noun, as in a skit. A Purim spiel is a satirical play poking fun at anything and everything.

That salesman has a convincing spiel.

Yenemsville

Wherever, from the Yiddish *yenem*, someone else, whoever.

Our babysitter went back to college. But we don't want to replace her with just *yenem*. We'll need to find someone experienced.

We got lost looking for a shortcut and wound up in Yenemsville.

In addition, there are some suffixes can turn English words into Yiddishisms:

-meister

Literally, master, as in the English word quizmaster. For example, a spinmeister is Yinglish for spin-doctor, someone who can give a positive interpretation to a negative event. A shlockmeister is a purveyor of shoddy goods.

-nik

Originally from Russian (as in Sputnik), the Yiddish suffix nik indicates that a person or thing is associated with something else. Alrightnik, nogoodnik, beatnik, peacenik fall into this category, as well as refusenik, a Jew who was refused an exit visa from the Soviet Union. It is also used in Modern Hebrew in the same way. *Seruvnik*, for example, is the Hebrew for refusnik;

a *Hashomer Hatza'irnik* is a member of the Young Guard, a left-leaning Zionist youth group; and a kibbutznik is a member of a kibbutz, a collective farm.

A nudnik is a pest, as in "I told you, I don't like South Park. Now stop trying to convince me to watch it. You're being a nudnik." It comes from the Yiddish *nudyn*, to bore. Alrightnik, a new immigrant who has done well for himself, comes from the Yinglish olreitnik and was used to refer to a smug upstart or braggart. A nogoodnik, a word first recorded in 1936, is the opposite of an alrightnik.

- tchik
From the Slavic, to indicate a diminutive. The most familiar example to English speakers is boychik, often used as a term of affection.

Hey, boychik, how's it going?

- shm
Adding "shm" to the beginning of the second word makes it into an object of derision

She thinks her retirement party is so fancy shmancy. I have seen more lavish birthday parties for two-year-olds.

Another Yiddishism is the doubling of words. Mishmash, which comes from *gemish*, the Yiddish word for mixture, is an example of doubling, as is pish-posh, a word that sounds Yiddish but is not.

There are many people who think they can sound as though they're speaking in a Yiddish accent by using a New York one. The two accents are not the same. Fran Drescher does not have a Yiddish accent; Fannie Brice did. (Actually, she didn't, but she used one on stage. In fact, she didn't even speak Yiddish. You can hear the difference when Barbra Streisand, who played Fannie Brice in *Funny Girl* and *Funny Lady*, is performing one of Brice's acts and when she's portraying Brice's private life.)

The classic Yiddish actress Molly Picon also had a Yiddish accent only on stage; she normally spoke unaccented English. Mel Brooks has one as the Two Thousand Year-Old Man and as Yogurt in *Spaceballs*; he doesn't have one in *High Anxiety*. In *Crossing Delancey*, the grandmother has a Yiddish accent; the granddaughter does not. James Cagney, who wasn't Jewish but could speak fluent Yiddish, had a New York accent.

A Yiddish accent is heavily inflected with Russian or German or Polish cadences and pronunciations. If someone is banging on the front door, a native English speaker might say: "I'm coming already. Hold your horses." A native Yiddish speaker might say: "Vas is der matter? A fire, God forbid? I'll be dere fast as I can. You can vait maybe a minute?"

When my mother's first cousins started kindergarten, their teachers thought they were immigrants because of their strong Yiddish accents, but they were born in Boston, not Eastern Europe (or, for that matter, New York). Their grandmother (my maternal great-grandmother), who spoke no English, lived with them and raised them while my great-aunt and -uncle worked in their deli. (For Bostonians-in-the-know, it was Andrew's Deli on Blue Hill Avenue in Roxbury.) My cousins had picked up my great-grandmother's accent - in fact, the younger cousin didn't speak any English - but quickly lost it once they were in school. Their adult accents were pure Bostonian.

According to my mother, I sounded like an immigrant when I was young, too, probably because we lived in the same house with my paternal great-grandmother, who arrived in the United States about twenty years earlier than my maternal one. We also lived across the street from my Eastern European-born maternal grandparents. (My paternal grandparents were both born in the United States.). My paternal great-grandmother, who lived in the U.S. for seventy years until she died at the age of ninety in 1969, always claimed, "I don't haff no haccent. I'm a Hamerican."

There are certain sentence structures that make people sound as though they are speaking Yiddish rather than English. For example, it is a characteristic quirk of Yiddish to answer a question with a question: "How are you?" "Nu, how should I be?"

Yiddish sentence structures include other syntactical devices, such as reversing the order of words ("A successful businessman he is not.") or placing the emphasis to indicate sarcasm or derision ("A businessman he thinks he is?")

Fans of *Star Wars* if you be, a Yiddish accent did not Yoda have, know you. But speak did he in sentence order reversed. (Go to: yodaspeak.co.uk to have more fun with Yoda.)

Many sentences sound as though the words are translated from Yiddish into their literal English equivalents, rather than into colloquial or conversational English. An example of literal translation can be seen in the use of "by" to mean "according to" or "with," as in "By you, a chiropractor is a doctor. By me, he's no doctor," or, "Don't worry about a babysitter. The children can stay by us." The Andrews Sisters in their hit song *Bei Mir Bist Du Shoen* (using the German spelling), literally translated as "By Me You Are Beautiful," made use of "by" in this way.

Bei Mir Bist Du Schoen, written by Jacob Jacobs (lyrics) and Sholom Secunda (music) for a long-forgotten 1932 Yiddish musical, was rediscovered in 1937 by lyricist Sammy Cahn, who heard it at the Apollo Theater in Harlem - sung in Yiddish by an African-American duo named Johnnie and George. The audience - and Cahn - loved the song. He obtained the rights, rewrote it with Saul Chaplin using English lyrics, and convinced the Andrew Sisters, who were Lutheran, to record it later that year.

There are other words that are not Yiddish, but sound as though they could be. There was a scene in the TV series The West Wing about words that should be Yiddish; among them were 'spatula' and 'farfetched."

Cockamamie
Inane, half-baked, silly

You're not painting your bedroom black. Wherever did you come up with such a cockamamie idea?

Some etymological dictionaries claim that "cockamamie" comes from decalcomania, a fad in the 1840s of decorating furniture - and skin - with decals. It had a revival more recently as decoupage and temporary tattoos.

Compote
A stew made of dried fruits such as apricots and prunes. The word is not Yiddish, but most Eastern European languages have cognates that mean the same thing.

We always have compote on Passover to counteract the effects of too much matzo.

Finagle
To cheat, to weasel out of. It sounds Germanic, but is American English, first used in 1926. It may come from the British dialectical word fainaigue, to cheat or renege at cards.

He tried to finagle his way out of our deal.

Kitsch
From the German word for gaudy, which is why it sounds Yiddish.

Those tchotchkes are kitschy.

Potrzebie

A made up word scattered throughout *Mad* Magazine.

My son's such a smart aleck. I asked him what he wants for his birthday, and he said, "A brand new potrzebie."

The word first appeared in the April, 1954, *Mad* Magazine letters column. Someone asked for the the meaning of furshlugginer, and the answer was, "It means the same as potrzebie."

The generally accepted story is that Harvey Kurtzman saw the Polish word *potrzeba*, meaning "something needed" or "a necessity" (possibly on a bottle of aspirin), and decided it would make a great nonsense word. But according to Al Jaffee, interviewed by Leah Garrett in the *Forward*, "There was an expression in Lithuania when I was a kid - *putz-rebbe*. Harvey must have heard that. Putz is genitals and it is applied as an insult to the rebbe. It's like saying, 'Oh that stupid teacher' or *putz-rebbe*."

Mad Magazine is filled with words that are either Yiddish (*ganef, farshluggine, farshimelt, shmendrick*) or sound as though they could be (veeblefetzer, feh, ech, shmeck, hoo ha). The writers used Yiddishisms for some of their great puns, like a satire of "Mandrake the Magician" called "Shmendrake the Magician," and a spin on the "I Like Ike" electioneering slogan: "I Like Lox."

Shtum

Quiet, still. Although it sounds Yiddish, the word is directly from the German word *stum*, silent. Also spelled "schtumm," "stumm," and "shtoom," its usuage is fairly recent and was originally used by the British criminal underground.

Stay *shtum* and maybe we will get away with it.

Shyster

A shady or dishonest lawyer.

He might be a shyster, but he always gets his clients off.

Although often referring to Jewish lawyers, the term "shyster" is used for any lawyer who is not quite kosher. The word comes from *sheis*, the German word for shit, which some may consider a rather appropriate etymology. The word may also be connected to Shylock, although Shakespeare's character was a moneylender, not a lawyer. The only lawyer in the play was Portia, whose name has become synonymous with "woman lawyer." Whether she was a shyster is a matter of interpretation and perspective.

Chapter Four

Iz Nisht Kosher
Words Familiar to English Speakers

Just as Yiddish-speakers who moved to English-speaking countries incorporated English words into Yiddish, so, too, did Yiddish words gradually become part of casual English vocabulary. In a reciprocal cultural exchange, non-Jewish English speakers now use many Yiddish words, sometimes without realizing their etymologies. Listen to the radio, go to a movie or play, watch a TV show, read a newspaper in print or online, check out the comic pages, surf the Internet, eavesdrop on a casual conversation, and you will hear Yiddish, whether in a metropolitan area with a large Jewish population or in an isolated rural community. Certain Yiddish words have become so commonly used in Standard English they are recognized by word processing programs as being spelled correctly. (Ones that are not accepted can lead to some amusing suggestions: "slipper" for shlepper, for example, "bubbles" for bupkis, "gaunt" for gezunt, its exact opposite.) The Yiddish words kosher (as in "That deal doesn't sound quite kosher to me."); chutzpah (classic definition: A man kills his parents and asks the judge for mercy because he's an orphan); shlep ("I can't believe my boss wants me to shlep all the way across town during rush hour to pick up a file that could be e-mailed;" or "How did you manage to shlep all those grocery bags up three flights of stairs?"); the derogatory shlemiel ("She had the chutzpah to try and fix me up with that shlemiel"); and the vulgarisms shmuck, putz, and drek have all made their way into English slang.

I. Yiddish words overheard being used by non-Jews

Both Jews and non-Jews sometimes use Yiddish words without knowing their actual meanings although most do use them appropriately See People Try to Define Yiddish Words (https://www.youtube.com/watch?v=w0WKYhkg lo.).

The ones below are some of the words I have overheard in conversation, read in news media or online, or heard in TV shows and movies, either expressed by non-Jews or intended for general audiences. (There are more detailed definitions of many of the words and their usages elsewhere in the book.)

Bupkis (Nothing)

The word is popular among comic strip creators. In the one-panel comic *Rubes*, two fish with feet are venturing out of the primordial ooze for the first time. One says, "What a disappointment. Here we are making history, and what do we get? Bupkis! No press conferences, no paparazzi, no parades…"

In another *Rubes*, Burt and Ernie of *Sesame Street* fame are duck hunting. Ernie says, "We've been here all day and what do we have to show for it? Bupkis."

And in a third *Rubes*, a gull is complaining that people get praised for picking up the litter on a beach once a year, while gulls clean up every day "and what do we get? Bupkis!"

In *Get Fuzzy*, the snarky Siamese cat tells his owner that "Alexander the Great had conquered the known world by the time he was your age. You haven't conquered bupkis."

On the TV show *Futurama*, a character that is a Jewish lobster commented, "We had four years of President Bush and what did we get? Bupkis."

Chutzpah (Guts, nerve, impudence)

The 2016 Presidential campaign featured many comments using the word chutzpah. For example, President Obama, talking about one of the GOP obstructionist members of Congress running for reelection: "This is now a guy who, because poll numbers are bad, has sent out brochures with my picture on them touting his cooperation on issues with me. Now that is the definition of chutzpah."

Garrison Keillor, talking about Chris Christie and Rudy Giuliani said, "This is a new level of chutzpah. This is like the captain of the Titanic, had he survived, writing a book about the art of navigation."

And then there was the time when GOP candidate Michele Bachmann mangled the pronunciation of chutzpah.

(https://www.youtube.com/watch?v=QB8iiIwUE
P0&autoplay=1

Drek (Shit)

At a meeting, a social worker who is Catholic said, while describing a cluttered house, "You wouldn't believe all the drek there."

An ad for tech services that ran on radio stations in Philadelphia and New York asked, "Are you tired of bosses who don't know the difference between high tech and drek?" I doubt the FCC would have allowed the ad if the line had been "...the difference between high tech and shit."

In the comic strip *Zits*, the parents of a fifteen-year-old boy find his computer open to his Facebook page and can't resist the temptation to peek.The mother says, "We shouldn't dignify this Facebook dreck [sic] with our attention."

Gai kak'n in dem yam (Go take a crap in the ocean.):

On the HBO series *Nurse Jackie*, a very brusque hospital administrator insincerely offers condolences to an elderly woman whose husband just died. The bereaved woman sweetly answers in Yiddish, *Gai kak'n in dem yam*. The administrator is told it means "Thank you."

Golem (a humanoid creature shaped from clay)

Referring to mainstream media, White supremacist and alt-right cofounder Richard B.

Spencer said, "One wonders if these people are people at all, or instead soulless *golems*."

Hak (pester)

In an article about traveling in Morocco, a blogger wrote: "Among the snake charmers and shop keepers, you'll also be *hocked* [sic] by women offering, some rather aggressively, to apply henna art to your hands."

Kosher (appropriate, legit)

On many British productions, particularly crime stories, it is common to hear warnings like, "You'd better stay shtum about the new TV; it isn't quite kosher.

Kvell (feel proud; boast)

On an NPR interview show, the interviewee said, "Come on, let me *kvell* a bit."

Kvetch (grumble, complain)

On Facebook, someone posted: "Excuse me while I indulge in a public kvetch. This has been a hell of a day."

In the comic strip *Speed Bump*, a cartoon of an elderly couple complaining about their aches and pains was captioned "Kvetch-22."

In another comic strip, *Free Range*, a dog owner throws a stick and says "Fetch." The dog begins a litany of complaints and the owner responds, "I said fetch! Not kvetch."

A TV critic for *Time* Magazine, writing about TV show Curb Your Enthusiasm, said "... back with presumably much to kvetch about."

L'chaim (To life.)
In an episode of *MASH*, a South Korean black marketeer made a toast: "L'chaim."

Megillah (story)
A review of the documentary *Inside Psycho* began with the sentence, "If you want to know the whole megillah about *Psycho* ..."

Meshuga (crazy)
Will Bunch, a columnist, writing about reforming the election process, criticized "the Electoral College that thwarted the majority will of 65 million Americans, and the meshuga tradition of voting on a regular workday, instead of on the weekend as in most civilized nations."

Mitzvah (good deed)
In a crime novel, *Glass Houses*, by Louise Penny, a Francophone Québécois police superintendent said about a group of women exiled to a remote island by the Inquisition where they cared for abandoned, disabled infants: "The witches did a mitzvah."

On Facebook, someone who received an unexpected favor posted: "Doesn't even seem real, does it? Such a mitzvah."

Nosh (To snack or munch)

A headline on a food page in a newspaper, talking about pre-sports game parties, said, "Have some time before the game? Nosh this."

Oy (Interjection signifying pain, weariness, disgust, resignation, etc.)

In the comic strip *Shoe*, a woman complains about the guy she's dating; "He puts the 'oy' in 'boyfriend.'"

Oy Vey (Oh, no.)

Variations on the interjection oy are used frequently in English. For example, an opinion column by Dana Milbank in the Washington Post was headlined "Oy Vey! Enough of Trump!"

Putzing (acting like a prick)

In the comic strip *Daddy's Home*, an angry son yells at his father to "stop putzing around" and then says, "In my defense, putzing doesn't even sound like a word."

Shlep (drag)

On *EastEnders*, a BBC nighttime soap opera, a character said about some strangers, "Why would someone shlep all the way over here?"

Shlong (penis)

In 2015, Trump said of Clinton, "... She was going to beat - she was favored to win - and she got schlonged. She lost. She lost."

Shlub (boor)

In the comic strip *The Duplex*, a character orders vanilla ice cream and the server says, "We go through the trouble of creating 31 flavors so some schlub [sic] can order 'vanilla'!"

Shmatte (rags)

Oprah, on her eponymous talk show, is discussing weight loss with Star Jones and says, "I guess you had to replace all your *shmattes*."

Shmooze (chat)

The earth's atmosphere has been poisoned by the Sontarans on the BBC science fiction show *Doctor Who*. The Doctor, a Time Lord from Gallifrey, is about to save the planet again, and says, "Are we going to stand around here shmoozing?"

Shmuck (asshole)

Would there have been a movie called *Dinner for Assholes*? But there was a popular one in 2010 titled *Dinner for Schmucks* [sic].

On *Wallender*, a British mystery series shown on PBS and starring an Irish-born actor playing a Swedish detective, one of the officers comments that a suspect is "such a shmuck."

In the movie *Goodfellas*, a character with a Jewish name says to the Italian gangsters, "Am I something special? Some sort of shmuck on wheels?"

Shmutz (dirt)

On a TV cooking competition, a chef with a Hispanic last name said it was important to leave enough time to plate your meal or it would look like "shmutz on a plate."

Shande (shame, embarrassment)

Peggy Noonan, Ronald Reagan's head speech writer and a Pultizer Prize winner for commentary, tweeted about the removal of stained glass windows commemorating Robert E. Lee and Stonewall Jackson from the National Cathedral. She called it "*a shonda*" [sic]. She was criticized not just for her cultural misappropriation of a Yiddish word, but for misspelling the transliteration.

Spiel (long-winded story)

At a meeting, a nurse who is a Hindu from Trinidad said, "I'm not going to bore you by going through the whole spiel."

Shtick (a stick, an act)

In a review of a TV series, a British tabloid wrote that a character's "misery-loves-company shtick" was getting boring.

Tuchus (ass)

In the comic strip *Close to Home*, Patrick Henry is quoted as saying, "Give me liberty or give me a good swift kick in the tuchus!"

In the comic strip *Bloom County*, Opus overreacts when he mistakes a piece of red licorice on his foot for a tick. The groundhog is carrying him and asks if he can put him down, "or do you have a piranha on your tuckus [sic]."

II. Other Commonly Used Words

There are many other words that are more-or-less familiar to English speakers. In addition to the words in this chapter, there are others elsewhere in the book.

Farshtaitz
Understand
I'm tired of repeating myself, so listen carefully. Farshtaitz?

Fumfn
To mumble, search for right word, also transliterated as fonfn.
He's a terrible public speaker. All he does is *fumfn*.
I can't believe Marlon Brando got such good reviews for *The Godfather*. I couldn't understand a word he said. All he did was *fumfn*.

Gezunt, Gezuntehait
Health
I don't care if the baby's a boy or girl as long as it is *gezunt*.
Abi gezunt. Be healthy.
It was great to see you again. *Abi gezunt*.
Abi gezunt - dos lebn ken men zikh alain nemen. Be well - you can kill yourself later.

I'm tired of listening to you complain about how terrible your life is. *Abi gezunt - dos lebn ken men zikh alain nemen.*

Gai gezsunt Go in health.

Mazel tov on your move. *Gai gezsunt.*

Gai gezuntehait Go in good health.

Are you finally leaving? *Gai gezuntehait.*

Gai gezunt un kum gezunt. Go in health and come in health. Have a wonderful trip.

Glitch

From the Yiddish word for "smooth, slippery," a glitch is when something has gone wrong, in the sense of "slipped up."

He refuses to take responsibility for his own actions and won't admit when he doesn't know how to do something. So whenever he messes up on the computer, he says there's a glitch in the software.

Mad Magazine's cartoonist Don Martin often used Yiddish words as sound effects. Glitch, for example, is the sound made by a shoe stepping in dog shit.

Haimish

Pronounced like a Scottish first name, *haimish* is the Yiddish word for a place that is welcoming, comfortable, and home-like.

The founders of that small startup company think they've created a *hamish* environment, but they're all a bunch of nudniks and busybodies.

Kibitz

Not to be confused with a kibbutz, an Israeli collective farm, kibitz is a nice way to say "gossip." Compare with shmooze and yenta

My sister drives me up the wall - she always seems to know when I'm busy and calls just to kibitz. Then she gets angry at me for wanting to hang up.

A kibitzer is someone who is a chatterbox, but is not quite so nosy a busybody as a yenta.

I bumped into my neighbor in the supermarket and could not get away from her. She had to tell me everything that's going on. What a kibitzer.

Klutz

Someone who is clumsy, a person who always trips or drops things. Not as out of control as a bull in a china shop, but you don't want to serve them dinner on your best dishes.

My sister is such a klutz, I think it'll make sense for me to use paper plates tonight.

L'chaim

As anyone who has seen *Fiddler on the Roof* knows, l'chaim means "to life." It is a toast in Hebrew, Yiddish, and, increasingly, English. It can also be used ironically.

Let's toast your new house! L'chaim!

So, you got away with cheating on the test? L'chaim.

Makher

Literally, a maker; refers to a big shot, a major player. The word is usually seen in English spelled with "ch," but it is pronounced with the gutteral "kh."

He thinks he's such a big *makher*, but he's just an assistant.

Maven

An expert. Can also be used sarcastically.

I can barely turn on the computer, but my ten-year old grandson-the-genius is a real maven.

He thinks he's such a maven, but talk to him for five minutes and you realize he doesn't know what he's talking about.

Zingn ken ikh nit, ober a maivin bin ikh. I can't sing, but I'm an expert. (Those who can, do; those who can't, criticize.)

Mazel tov

Literal translation is "good luck," but used as "congratulations." Can be used ironically

So, you finally decided to come visit your mother? Mazel tov!

Mensch

Literally, a man, but used to refer to a particular type of man, one who has a good heart and puts others first.

If he'd been a mensch, he'd have offered to use his snow blower on his neighbors' driveway. But he didn't.

As an adjective, the word is *menschlich*. *Menschlichkeit* describes the essence of what a mensch is.

I heard you took up a collection to buy Christmas gifts for your neighbor's kids when he got laid off. That was a menschlich thing to do.

It is *menschlichkeit* to do things because they are the right things to do, not because you want to get recognition for doing them.

Minyan

The quorum of ten adults required to have a full prayer service.

The members of the synagogue are getting older, and their kindelakh are moving to newer neighborhoods. They couldn't read the Torah today because they didn't have a minyan.

The minyan used to consist only of men over the age of thirteen. Beginning in the late 1950s, women began to be counted as well. Now all but the most traditional synagogues include women in the minyan.

Moyel

The person who makes the male *kindelakh* Jewish, the ritual circumciser who officiates at the bris (circumcision) of an eight-day-old infant boy or of an adult male convert to Judaism. The word is sometimes seen spelled as mohel.

I thought the father was going to faint when he saw the *moyel* approach his baby with a scalpel.

Queen Victoria believed her family descended from King David, and decreed that her son Prince Albert was to be circumcised in accordance with Jewish tradition. Since then, until the latest generation, the British royal family has always used a moyel. Prince Charles was circumcised by Rabbi Jacob Snowman, official Mohel of the London Jewish community. His children, however, were not snipped, possibly because Princess Diana was opposed to the practice, which is out-of-fashion in England.

Nebbish; nebekh

An ineffectual guy, a nobody; the Anglicized version of nebekh.

I don't understand what she sees in such a nebbish. Not only does he have the personality of a blank piece of paper, but he can't even hold down a job.

He just got fired as a shelf stocker at the convenience store. Nebekh!

Nu

An untranslatable interjection, similar to "So?"

Your landlord is increasing your rent? Nu, what do you plan to do now?

Plotz

Literally, to explode, but not in the sense of anger. It has a connotation of collapsing.

I'm going to plotz from all the work I have to do.

I could have plotzed when I heard my favorite store went bankrupt.

Shabbos
Sabbath, the Day of Rest, from sundown Friday night until sundown Saturday.

He says he observes Shabbos, but I saw him go into a Dunkin' Donuts on the way home from shul.

Shabbos goy
A non-Jew hired to do the tasks forbidden on the Sabbath

The synagogue president was a hypocrite. He insisted they hire a Shabbos goy to open up and close the shul, but he drove to services.

Traditionally observant Jews refrain from doing any work, including cooking, carrying objects outside the home, sewing, driving, or using electricity, which includes turning lights on and off. Some tear toilet paper before Shabbos begins, and unscrew the bulb in the refrigerator so it does not turn on when the door is opened. In order to turn lights on and off either at home or in the synagogue, a non-Jew would be hired to do those tasks. This person was called a Shabbos goy.

There are several prominent individuals who were Shabbos goyim [the plural] when they were young. Elvis Presley was so happy to help Rabbi Albert Fruchter of Memphis keep Shabbos that he refused to accept any money from him. General Colin Powell, who grew up in the South Bronx and spoke Yiddish, earned a quarter for turning the lights on and off in an Orthodox synagogue on Friday nights. Former New York governor Mario Cuomo has said of his parents' friends the Kesslers, "I was a Shabbos goy because of them." When both Al Gore and Joe Lieberman were in the Senate together, Gore acted as Lieberman's Shabbos goy. When Lieberman would stay overnight in his office so he could cast votes on Shabbos, Gore would come in to turn the lights on and off for him.

Shlemiel

A dorky guy

He's such a shlemiel, I can't imagine fixing him up with any of my friends. They'd never speak to me again!

Shlimazel

A guy who never gets a break.

What a shlimazel - he quit his job when he thought he had a new one, and before he started working there, the company went bankrupt.

A shlimazel falt oyfen ruken un tzeklapt zich dem noz. A shlimazel falls on his back and hits his nose.

A classic example of the difference between a shlemiel and a shlimazel: A shlemiel spills his soup; a shlimazel is the one he spills it on.

Many Americans are familiar with the words schlemiel and schlimazel from the jump rope rhyme heard at the beginning of the TV show *Laverne and Shirley*: "One, two, three, four, five, six, seven, eight. Schlemiel, schlimazel, Hasenfeffer incorporated."

Shlep; shlepper; shleppy
To drag around.
My mother made me shlep her all over town looking for a blouse to match a skirt that didn't look good on her anyway.
A shlepper can be a gofer, but he can also be someone who lacks ambition, is a hanger-on.
According to Hollywood, if you're bright and get a job as a shlepper in a warehouse, you'll eventually marry the boss's daughter and take over the company.
She married a real shlepper. He always has excuses for not finding a job.
The adjective shleppy describes someone who is disheveled, slovenly.
Put on a clean shirt. You look shleppy.

Shlock
Cheaply made goods. Also used for bad or trashy entertainment.
I can't believe you spent good money for that shlock.
Why are you watching that shlock? Put on PBS instead.

Shlub
Sounds like slob, and that's what a shlub is. Usually someone slovenly, ill mannered, coarse, boorish. Sometimes transliterated as zhlub.
Homer Simpson is a loveable shlub.

Shlump, shlumper, shlumpy; shlumperdik
Disheveled, messy

He is a big guy, but he doesn't look like a shlump. He is always well groomed.

My neighbor sits out on the front steps in a dirty t-shirt drinking beer from the bottle. He is a real shlumper.

That sweater is too big on you. It looks shlumpy.

We are going out to dinner with Bubbe and Zaide. Go put on a clean shirt. You look shlumperdik.

Shmooze

Similar to kibitz, but more in the sense of aimless chatting than gossiping.

Forget about "If you snooze, you lose." In this job, if you shmooze, you lose.

Shmutz; shmutzik

Dirt. Can refer to physical or metaphorical dirt

Who tracked that shmutz onto my clean floor?

I don't care if they do publish literary articles. *Playboy* is still shmutzik.

Shnorrer

A beggar, a panhandler, someone looking to get something for nothing. Can also be a professional fundraiser.

That *shnorrer* is always asking me to drive him to work, but he never offers to chip in for gas.

Don't bother returning her call. She is just *shnorring* for some charity or other.

In the 1930 movie Animal Crackers. Groucho Marx rhymed *shnorrer* with "explorer" during the song *Hooray for Captain Spaulding*. The song later became the theme for his TV game show *You Bet Your Life*.

Shrek, shreklikh

Horror, a fright. Not to be confused with shriek, although a shrek can cause you to do so. Also not to be confused with the anti-Disney character of the same name, whose creators undoubtedly were familiar with the Yiddish word.

My teenaged son's room is shreklikh. It's a health hazard.

Shtick

A piece. The word is sometimes spelled shtik, but computer programs do not recognize that spelling.

She's fooled herself into thinking that if she breaks up the candy bar into small shticks, there won't be as many calories. No wonder she keeps gaining weight.

In English, shtick often refers to a particular trait or mannerism.

I know it's just her shtick, but it drives me crazy when she always has to hug everyone.

It can also refer to a stand-up comedian's act or an actor's typical role.

Owen Wilson always plays the same kind of slightly goofy, sensitive male character. It's his shtick.

Don Rickle's shtick was to insult people.

The suffix "l" or "el" transforms a noun into a diminutive. The addition of "leh" makes the word into a super-diminutive. For example, a *shtikl* is a small piece of something and a *shtikeleh* is even smaller.

How do you know you don't like broccoli if you won't try it? Here, just taste a *shtikeleh*.

Shul

Synagogue. From the German word for school, as a synagogue is also a place of study.

My neighbor always says he goes to shul religiously and laughs as though he's so clever.

Shvitz

A steam bath.

My grandfather used to go out on Thursday nights with "the boys" to sit in the *shvitz*, smoke cigars, play pinochle, and shmooze. It was the highlight of his week.

As a verb, it means to sweat.

The air conditioning is broken and I can't stop *shvitzing*.

A *shvitzer* is not necessarily someone who is perspiration challenged, but a braggart.

That *shvitzer* I work with had to make sure everyone knew he got a new sportscar.

Tchotchke
Bauble, worthless item, a dust catcher.

My Enterprise Christmas tree ornament is not a tchotchke. It's a rare and valuable *Star Trek* collectible.

Tzuris
Trouble.

First she lost her job, then her dog died, and now she has the flu. I have never seen one person have so much *tzuris* all at once.

Yenta
A busybody, a gossip.

I'd never tell her a secret. She is such a yenta.

Riddle: What business is a Yenta in? Yours.

Yeshiva
Generally, a religious school for advanced study. Also the name of a Jewish university in New York City.

A young man who attends a traditional yeshiva is a yeshiva *bokher* (yeshiva boy or bachelor).

He's a yeshiva *bokher*, so he'll need to find a wife who will be able to support the family.

Chapter Five

Vi Iz Ei'er Nomen?
What's in a Name?

There's an old bi-lingual joke. (To understand it, you need to know the Yiddish words *fargessen* means "forgotten" and *shoyn* means "already.") A recently arrived Jewish immigrant from Eastern Europe settled on the Lower East Side of New York and introduced himself to his neighbors as Sean Fergusson. "Sean Fegusson?" one exclaimed. "What kind of name is that for a nice Jewish boy?"

The man explained: "Before I bought my ticket for the ship, my neighbor told me, 'You can't go to America with a name like yours. You need a simple American name. Tell them your name is John Smith.' When I bought the ticket and the clerk asked me my name, I said, *'Shoyn fergessen,'* and that's what he wrote down."

It's widely but erroneously believed that the immigration officials at Ellis Island changed Jewish names to be more Anglo-sounding. In actuality, the officials copied the names directly from the ships' manifests, which were compiled at the points of embarkation. The name changes, therefore, were made either by shipping officials in Europe, by the families themselves before they bought their tickets, or, more often, by the individuals when they later applied for their naturalization papers.

Many Jews Anglicized their names, and not just to assimilate. For example, many a Fox was born Fuchs (pronounced fyooks), but changed the name so as to avoid the inevitable mispronunciation and subsequent teasing. But others, particularly those in show business, did change their names so they would be more "acceptable" to goyishe America.

Here is a far from complete list:

Woody Allen …Allen Stewart Koenigsberg
June Allyson…Ella Geisman
Lauren Bacall…Betty Joan Perske
Jack Benny…Benjamin Kubelsky
Milton Berl…Mendel Berlinger
Irving Berlin…Israel Baline
Joey Bishop…Joseph Gottleib
Karen Black…Karen Blanche Ziegler
Michael Bolton…Michael Bolotin
Victor Borge…Borge Rosenbaum
Fanny Brice…Fanny Borach
Mel Brooks…Melvin Kaminsky
George Burns…Nathan Birnbaum
Red Buttons…Aaron Chwatt
Eddie Cantor…Edward Israel Iskowitz
Mama Cass…Ellen Cohen
Jeff Chandler…Ira Grossel
Lee J.Cobb…Amos Jacob
Tony Curtis…Bernard Schwartz
Rodney Dangerfield…Jacob Cohen
Kirk Douglas…Isser Danielovitch Demsky
Melvyn Douglas…Melvyn Hesselberg
Bob Dylan…Robert Zimmerman
Kenny G…Ken Gorelick

Paulette Goddard...Marion Levy
Elliot Gould...Elliot Goldstein
Lee Grant...Lyova Geisman
Laurence Harvey Laruschka Mischa Skikne
Judy Holliday...Judith Tuvim
Houdini...Erich Weiss
Sam Jaffe...Shalom Jaffe
Al Jolson...Asa Yoelson
Danny Kaye...Daniel Kaminsky
Michael Landon...Michael Orowitz
Steve Lawrence...Sidney Leibowitz
Jerry Lewis...Joseph Levitch
Peter Lorre...Lazlo Lowenstein
Barry Manilow...Barry Pincus
Ross Martin...Martin Rosenblatt
Elaine May...Elaine Berlin
Yves Montand...Ivo Levy
Paul Muni...Meshilem Meier Weisenfreund
Mike Nichol...Michael Peschkowsky
Stephanie Powers...Stephanie Federkrewcz
Joey Ramone...Jeffrey Hyman
Joan Rivers...Joan Molinsky
Edward G. Robinson...Emanuel Goldenberg
Jane Seymour Joyce Penelope Frankenburg
Simone Signoret   Simone Kaminker
Beverly Sills...Belle Silverman
Harold J.Stone...Harold Jacob Hochstein
Sophie Tucker...Sophia Kalish
Gene Wilder...Gerald Silberman
Natalie Wood...Natasha Gurdin

Not every actor changed to a more "American"-sounding name. For example, Tovah Feldshuh was born Terri Sue. For a while she acted under the name Terri Fairchild, but then decided to use her Hebrew first name and original last name.

Originally, Jews did not have surnames, but were known by patronymics. Dovid, whose father's name was Shmuel, was called Dovid ben Shmuel. In English, his name would be David Samuelson.

In 1787, the Austrian Empire issued a decree ordering Jews to register with surnames taken from the German language. Napoleon in 1808 decreed that Jews adopt fixed names, to assist with census taking and tax collection. Similar laws were passed in Prussia in 1812, Poland in 1821, and Russia in 1844.

According to some sources (but not substantiated in others), Jews had to pay a registration fee, and those who could not afford to pay were assigned offensive or derogatory names, while the wealthy would be given pleasant names, like Rosenfeld (field of roses). The name Spater (later) was often given to Jews who were late in registering.

Most names were patronymics (Shuelovitz - Saul's son), occupations (Schneider - tailor), hometowns (Litwack - one from Lithuania), or physical characteristics (Klein - small). But whether or not it is true that officials gave silly-sounding names to the poor, those names can be found in many lists, even if they are no longer in use. Among them are:

Affengesicht (monkey face)
Auksenschvantz (ox tail)

Azelkopf (donkey head)
Bettelarm (destitute)
Billig (cheap)
Bleichfrosch (pale frog)
Deligtisch (criminal)
Drachenblut (dragon's blood)
Dreyfus (third foot, euphemism for penis)
Durst (thirst)
Fresser (glutton)
Galgenstrich (gallows rope, slang for a rogue)
Galgenvogel (gallows bird)
Gottlos (godless)
Groberklotz (roughneck)
Geschwur (ulcer)
Harn (urine)
Hazenfartz (rabbit face)
Hazenshprung (rabbit leap)
Hinterkop (back of the head)
Hunger (hunger)
Kaker (crapper)
Kanalgeruch (sewer stink)
Karfunkel (carbuncle)
Küssemich (kiss me)
Ladstockschwinger (ramrod swinger)
Langnuz (long nose)
Lumpe (crook, rag)
Maulthier (mule)
Maulwurf (mole)
Nachtkäfer (night beetle)
Nashorn (rhinoceros)
Niemand (no one)
Nothleider (being needy)

Pferd (horse)

Pulverbestandtheil (powder component

Rindskopf (cow's head)

Säuger (suckler)

Saumagen (stomach of a female pig)

Schlanger (from shlong, euphemism for penis)

Shleicher (crawl)

Schmukler (from shmuk, euphemism for penis)

Schmutzbank (dirty bank)

Stinker (bad smelling)

Tannenbaum (fir tree, usually refers to a Christmas tree)

Taschengreifer (pickpocketer)

Todtzchläger (cudgel)

Trinker (drinker)

Unglick (misfortune)

Wanzenknicker (bug crusher)

Wanzreich (rich in bugs).

Authors sometimes give their Jewish characters names that are vulgar, coarse or insulting, usually used for comedic effect. The first was Shylock, in Shakespeare's *Merchant of Venice*. When Shakespeare named his character Shylock, the name was not yet a synonym for usurer, but was in use with that meaning within a century.

In his 1896 novel, *Leib Weihnachtzkuchen and His Child*, set in Galicia, author Karl Emil Franzos named his protagonist Weihnachtzkuchen, Christmas Cake.

In contemporary times, Woody Allen's stories, especially the later ones, contain names, many in English, which broadcast a character's personality or occupation; for example, Wiseman for a rabbi, Peplum for a tailor, or Fleshpot for a femme fatale. Others of Allen's surnames are Yiddish (or Yiddish-sounding) words, also used for satirical purposes. Among them are Bidnik, Eppis, Goldworm, Kugelmass, Mandelstam, Pinchuk, Schmeed, Schmeederer, Sheigitz, Untermensch, Varnishke, and Zipsky.

Several fictional names (some from published works) became part of colloquial Yiddish. Most of them refer to fools:

Chaim Yankel: A fool, a bumpkin

Chelmner: The fictional residents of the real Polish town of Chelm were known as the epitome of foolishness. Stories about "the wisemen of Chelm" are still popular folktales.

Kuni Lemel: An ineffectual fool, made famous in a series of eponymous plays and Israeli movies (*The Two Kuni Lemels*, *Kuni Lemel in Tel Aviv*, *Kuni Lemel in Cairo*)

Moyshe Kapoyer: One who does everything backwards. Created by humor columnist B. Kovner for the *Forvertz*.

Moyshe Pupik: Someone with an exaggerated and unwarranted image of himself. The name may have evolved from a nickname for an actual man named Moyshe who had a large stomach and larger ego.

Moyshe Zugmir: Literally, "Moses Tell-Me;" figuratively, "John Doe" or "Whatshisname?

Chapter Six

Freg Mikb'Kherem
Outside The Pale

In 1791, Catherine the Great established the Pale of Settlement as the area of Russia in which Jews were allowed to live. Comprising twenty percent of European Russia and located on its western side stretching to Central Europe, the Pale roughly corresponded to the modern borders of Lithuania, Poland, Ukraine, Moldavia, Belarus, and parts of western Russia. Ninety percent of Russian Jews resided within the Pale. Not only were they subject to discrimination and restrictions, being taxed at a higher rate and forbidden from owning land, but also the high concentration of their population in a limited space made them more easily subject to pogroms. Under the May Laws of 1882, they were further restricted to urban areas only. Not coincidentally, it was around this time that Jewish emigration to the United States increased dramatically, with an estimated two million settling in the United States from 1881-1914.

"I look upon you, sir, as a man who has placed himself beyond the pale of society, by his most audacious, disgraceful, and abominable public conduct." - *The Pickwick Papers*, Charles Dickens, 1837.

The phrase "outside the Pale" refers to an area outside of which local laws do not apply.

Figuratively, "outside the Pale," has come to refer to The Other, to anyone who is not part of the normative community standards of behavior or belief. Despite popular thought, the etymology of the phrase "outside the Pale" most likely comes not from the Jewish Pale of Settlement in Russia but from the English Pale in Ireland, an area of the island that came under the direct influence of England from the Thirteenth to the Sixteenth Centuries.

Ghetto

The origin of the word ghetto and the concept and the reality of the word are Italian, as Venice was the site of the first ghetto. It referred originally to a segregated neighborhood where Jews were required to reside. Now it is used for any restricted neighborhood, whether de jure (as in Apartheid-era South Africa) or de facto (as in the Gilded Ghettos where many affluent Americans live; for example, "Beverly Hills is a Gilded Ghetto.")

Pogrom

Not a Yiddish word, but used almost exclusively to refer to acts of violence against Jews. The word comes from Russian *pogromu*, "through acts of violence." The word is used for officially sanctioned riots, rampages, murders, rapes, and arsons perpetrated by the goyim against the Jews living in shtetls (small towns), large cities, ghettos, or anywhere else they resided and were persecuted.

In April 1903, on Easter weekend in Kishinev, then the capital of Bessarabia and now of Moldavia, forty-nine Jews were killed, almost six hundred were wounded, ninety-four of them seriously, and over seven hundred houses looted and destroyed during a pogrom. It was instigated by rumors published in local newspapers that the Jews had murdered a Christian boy in order to use his blood to make matzo.

Such accusations are called blood libels. They disregard the fact that Jewish dietary laws prohibit the eating of any blood, and to be considered kosher, animals must be salted and soaked in order to ensure that no blood remains.

The *New York Times*, which exaggerated the extent of the casualties, reported on April 28, 1903, in an article called "Jewish Massacre Denounced," on page 6: "The anti-Jewish riots in Kishinev, Bessarabia, are worse than the censor will permit to publish. There was a well laid-out plan for the general massacre of Jews on the day following the Russian Easter. The mob was led by priests, and the general cry, 'Kill the Jews,' was taken up all over the city. The Jews were taken wholly unaware and were slaughtered like sheep. The dead number 120 and the injured about 500. The scenes of horror attending this massacre are beyond description. Babes were literally torn to pieces by the frenzied and bloodthirsty mob. The local police made no attempt to check the reign of terror. At sunset the streets were piled with corpses and wounded. Those who could make their escape fled in terror, and the city is now practically deserted of Jews."

Blood libels have continued into the new millennium. In April, 2008, posters appeared in Novosibirsk, the third largest city in Russia, warning parents about the approach of Passover: "These vermin [Jews] are still performing rituals, stealing small children and draining their blood to make their sacred bread."

Shtetl
Small town, village. The word is a diminutive of the German *stadt*, state

The shtetl in Poland my great-grandparents came from no longer exists.

We live in a shtetl of Boston.

I. What They Call Us

Anti-Semitism is not manifested only through pogroms. Offensive words broadcast hatred as much as physical violence.

Christ Killer
It was not until the Second Vatican Council in 1965 that the Jews were officially absolved of responsibility for the Crucifixion. The expression, however, is still heard, and the sentiment behind it is still existent.

Four Wheel

The phrase is British, and comes from Cockney rhyming slang: "Four wheel skid" is shorthand for Yid.

Hymie

A disparaging name when used by goyim, unless it is someone's nickname. It comes from the Hebrew name Chaim, often Anglicized as Hyman.

Kike

Probably the best-known odious name, the word comes from *keikl*, the Yiddish word for circle. There are several different theories about its etymology:

In Medieval Germany, Jews were required to wear a yellow circle on the shoulder of their coats.

Jewish immigrants to the United States who did not know how to write their names in English signed with a circle instead of an X, which reminded them of a cross.

New immigrants to the United States who were mentally deficient had a chalk circle drawn on their clothing.

According to the Oxford English Dictionary, the etymology of the word is the commonly used suffixes -(s)ky or -(s)ki in Jewish surnames.

Pope Clement VIII (1536-1605) denounced the "blind (caeca in Latin) obstinacy" of the Jews.

Jewish clothing manufacturers were accused of making cheap copies of haute couture after having "peeped" at the designs. The German word "to peep" is *kieken*.

The term may be an acronym for "Christ Killer" (K.K.)

Sheeny

The etymology is unknown, but the word may come from the Yiddish *shaine*, beautiful. Jews often use the adjective, sometimes admiringly and sometimes ironically:

Such a *shaine maidl* (pretty girl) should have no problem getting a date for the prom.

Hey, *shaine punim* (beautiful face), stop futzing around with your hair and get to work.

Henry Ford was a noted anti-Semite. In 1919, he purchased the *Deerborn Independent*, and in his weekly column "Mr. Ford's Page," expounded his views that a Jewish conspiracy led by financiers was responsible for World War I. In 1920, his newspaper began a series called "The International Jew: The World's Problem," which ran for the next eighteen months. The columns were later collected in a book, in which he accused the Jews of undermining the Chrisitan world for financial profit. He even believed that Woodrow Wilson took secret orders from Supreme Court Justice Brandeis.

Ford believed the *Protocols of the Elders of Zion* was a blueprint for Jewish domination of the world. The book, supposedly based on a series of lectures by a Jewish scholar outlining the plans for the Jews to overthrow the European countries, was in fact a forgery created by the Secret Service of the Russian czar at the beginning of the Twentieth Century. Despite its being a complete fabrication, the book is still in circulation and accepted today by enemies of the Jews as fact.

In 1924, Ford was exposed in a Yiddish book called *Der Emes Vegen Henri Ford* (The Truth about Henry Ford), written by David Louis Meckler. In an agreement Ford signed with Louis Marshall of the American Jewish Committee, he declared he was "mortified" to learn the *Protocols* were a forgery, and said he would cease to publish anti-Semitic articles in the *Independent*, which he closed in 1927. Yet he later claimed someone had forged his signature on the agreement, and further asserted Jewish bankers were responsible for World War II.

To this day, there are many Jews who will not buy Ford automobiles because of his beliefs.

This is a popular joke based on Ford's views:

The three Goldberg brothers, Norman, Hyman, and Max invented the first automobile air-conditioner. They visited Ford and convinced him to come out to their car. It was a hot day, and the inside of the car was even hotter.

When they turned on the air-conditioner, the car cooled off immediately.

Ford offered them three million dollars for the patent. They said they would settle for two million, but only if they received recognition by having the label "The Goldberg Air-Conditioner" affixed to the dashboard of every car in which it was installed.

There was no way Ford was going to agree to having the Jewish name Goldberg emblazoned on two million cars that carried the Ford name. After several hours of negotiations, it was finally agreed that Ford would pay them four million dollars for the patent and that just their first names would be shown.

And so, even today, all Ford air-conditioners show on the controls, the names "Norm, Hi, & Max".

II. What We Call Them

Unfortunately, victims of bigotry can also be prejudiced. Yiddish has many derogatory words for anyone who's not Jewish.

Golakh
A monk. It means "smooth" and refers to the tonsure.

Is it true brandy was invented by a *golakh*?

Goy
From the Hebrew word for "nation," a goy is any non-Jew. The word is not always used only as a description or as a compliment.

What can you expect from the goyim?

Goyishe kop
Literally, a gentile head. It is not a description of someone with straight blonde hair

and a small nose. It refers to someone who lacks common sense and is not too bright.

She sent out her resume without proofreading, and it was full of typos. What do you expect from a *Goyishe kop*?

Nitelnacht

Literally, birth night; Yiddish word for Christmas Eve; related to "natal." Because Jews do not believe the messiah ("Christ" in Greek; *moshiakh* in Yiddish) has arrived, they avoid Yiddish words that would imply that he has.

Jews traditionally celebrate *Nitelnacht* by going out for Chinese food and a movie.

Shaigitz

The word for non-Jewish man. Unlike the word *shiksa*, which can sometimes be a compliment, *shaigitz* is always used disparagingly. It has a connotation of someone who is lower class, unsophisticated, uneducated.

The plural is *shkotzim*, a word that sounds as disdainful as it means. A *shkutz* is a boor. The word comes from the Hebrew, in the Book of Genesis, for creepy crawlies.

It was bad enough she married a goy, but she had to go marry a *shaigitz* who deals drugs.

The *shkutz* next door sits on his front steps drinking beer in his undershirt.

Shiksa

A non-Jewish woman. The word can be used derisively or admiringly.

I have to admit she is a good wife to him. I just wish she weren't a *shiksa*.

The blonde *shiksa* goddess is the dream of every Jewish nebbish from Philip Roth to Woody Allen to Ben Stiller.

Shvartze

Black. Well before coloreds became blacks, Jews called African-Americans shvartzes. The word was used descriptively not pejoratively. It is also the word for the color black. Nevertheless, it is seldom heard these days, as some think of it as being a derogatory or offensive word.

She's got such a tan she looks like a shvartze.

My great-great grandfather had black hair, so he was named Schwartz.

Often, it referred to the janitor in an apartment building or a cleaning woman:

Don't try to fix the light yourself. Let the shvartze do it.

The house is a mess. I am so glad the shvartze is coming today.

In *Blazing Saddles*, Mel Brooks, playing an Indian Chief, comes across a wagon with a black family. He speaks to them in Yiddish and allows them to leave. What he says is:

"Shvartzes!" [Blacks!]

(To an Indian threatening the family): "*Zai nit meshuga! Loz im gai'n!*" (Don't be crazy! Let them go!)

(To family): "*Abi gezunt!*" ("Be healthy!")

(To others): "*Hos di gezain in deine lebn*?" (Have you ever seen anything like this in your life?)

(In English) "They darker than us!"

The word can also refer to a calamity, as in the English expression "It is a black day,"

Last year was a *shvartz yor ahf mir* (a bad year for me). I was diagnosed with cancer. But *barukh hashem* (thank God), I am fine now.

Sylvesternacht; Sylvester

Literally, Sylvester's Eve; refers to New Year's Eve. Because the holiday of Rosh Hashanah begins the Jewish year, and December 31 in the Church calendar is dedicated to Saint Sylvester, Jews in Israel still call the secular New Year's Day Sylvester.

Our best friends are having a party for *Sylvesternacht*.

Yishka

Little Jesus, diminutive form of Yishu, Jesus, used to emphasize his Jewish birth while demeaning his importance. Sometimes called Yoshkele.

III. What we call ourselves

Jews are just as hard on themselves as non-Jews. But, as with any group, we can call each other names that would be anti-Semitic if said by a non-Jew.

In the insular and isolated world of the shtetl, to become non-observant was almost as bad as converting to Christianity.

In the United States today, there are many "flavors" of Judaism. Traditional Jews alone can be divided into Orthodox, Modern Orthodox, and Chasidic, subdivided again into several Chasidic sects, each following the teachings of a different rabbinic authority. Other movements, official or not, are Conservadox (more traditional than Conservative but not as much as Orthodox), Conservative, Reconstructionist, Reform, Renewal, Secular, Humanistic.

Although the Reform and Conservative movements began in the mid-Nineteenth Century in Germany, they flourished in the United States. In Eastern Europe, there were really only two choices: to be observant or secular. There were no shades of gray. You were either observant or non-observant.

In the Eighteenth Century, there was a new, revolutionary movement in the Jewish world of Eastern Europe: the Chasidim. Founded by the Ba'al Shem Tov (the Master of the Good Name), the movement emphasized joyous, spiritual, spontaneous prayer and observance, rather than the dry legalistic pieties of the scholarly rabbinic authorities in the Yeshivas of the day. The Ba'al Shem Tov taught that even the uneducated had the ear of God, and that one did not have to be a yeshiva bokher to experience God. The holders of the status quo, the leaders of the Yeshivas, were called *Misnagdim*, opponents.

It is ironic that the Chasidim are now regarded as the most stringent of traditional Jews. But they still believe in song and dance as paths to God.

The two groups temporarily ceased their animosity in the face of a common enemy: haskalah, the Enlightenment. The haskalah, beginning in the late Eighteenth Century in Germany, marked a movement toward increasing contacts between the Jewish communities and the "outside" world. It led the way toward secularization and the development of more liberal religious movements.

Apikoros
A heretic.
What do you mean you want to study Spinoza? He was an *apikoros*.

Kherem
Excommunication
What are you doing? If anyone sees you smoking on Shabbos, you'll be in *kherem*.
Freg mikh b'kherem. - Ask me in kherem. [How should I know?]
The most famous person to be placed in *kherem* was the philosopher Baruch Spinoza, because of his rationalistic philosophy and enlightened approach to the Bible.
Kherem was a very real threat to a Jew in the shtetl. Someone placed in *kherem* could be part of no community at all if shunned by other Jews. Unless the person in *kherem* converted to

Christianity, there would be no acceptance by the general population either.

Today, *kherem* is not a threat except to the most Orthodox. In 1945, Rabbi Mordecai M. Kaplan, the founder of Reconstructionist Judaism, was placed in *kherem* by the Union of Orthodox Rabbis, following the publication of Kaplan's new prayer book which rejected the supernaturalism of God and the chosenness of the Jewish people. He was quoted in the *Time* Magazine of June 25, 1945, as responding: "As I am not a member, I was excommunicated from nothing." He said further that the rabbis were "merely making themselves ridiculous ... The Union ... speaks in medieval terms."

Oysvorf
Literally, an outcast, a scoundrel, a non-conformist.

If you keep talking like an *apikoros*, you'll be an *oysvorf*.

Shaigetz einer
Literally, a true non-Jew; refers to an irreligious Jew.

I saw that *shaigetz einer* next door eating pork - and on Yom Kippur no less!

Traifener kop
Literally, a non-kosher head, the phrase refers to a non-observant Jew.

That *traifener kop* hasn't stepped inside a synagogue since he turned thirteen.

Someone who comes from the same area as you is a landsman, a countryman. Landsmen banded together in the United States to help one another become acclimated to the *Goldene Medina* (the Golden State - not California, but the United States). Their organizations, called landsmanshaften, gave financial aid and advice to the greeners (greenhorns) who quickly discovered that the streets were paved with cobblestones, mud, and horseshit, not gold. Anyone who came from the same area was automatically a landsman. Anyone else was considered inferior. The following words have two meanings. For those who came from these places, they were a badge of pride; for others, a term of derision.

Ashkenazi

All Jews of Central or Eastern European descent, as opposed to the Sephardim, those who trace their roots to the Iberian peninsula pre-1492. Ashkenazim consider Sephardim to be uncultured shepherds and Sephardim consider Ashkenazim to be uncultured religious fanatics. As with any stereotypes, both are right and both are wrong.

Galitzianer

Galitzia was the section of Eastern Europe that was part of the Austro-Hungarian Empire from 1772, when it was partitioned from Poland, until the end of World War I, when it was ceded back to the newly reestablished state of Poland. In 1945, it was divided between Poland, controlled by the Soviet Union, and Ukraine, occupied by the Soviets. After the fall of the Soviet system, Ukraine and Poland became independent again. Galitzianers were considered inferior by the Litvaks, who thought of them as boorish and sentimental.

Litvak

Litvaks came from the area around Lithuania and Latvia. Borders being fluid, people from current day Russia, Poland, Belarus and other countries were Litvaks. Litvaks were considered inferior by Galitzianers, who thought of them as humorless and doctrinaire.

Vos-Vos

A derogatory term in popular use after World War II for a Yiddish speaker, used by those who did not speak Yiddish, such as Israelis or assimilated English-speakers. It comes from such Yiddish expressions as *Far vos*? ("What for?") or *Vos iz dokh*? ("What is that?").

Yekke

If there is one thing Galitizianers and Litvaks can agree on, it is that no one likes *Yekkes*. They are the upper class, assimilated German Jews who have adopted the German characteristics of frugality, cleanliness, and inflexibility. They are the WASPS of the Jewish world.

Yid

Literally, Jew. Used by non-Jews in a derogatory manner, but descriptively by Jews.

Yiddishkeit means Jewishness in all its manifestations, particularly cultural.

They are not observant, but they still have that and there's a lot of Yiddishkeit in their home.

Pintele Yid

Point of light, spark of Jewishness

Vos macht a Yid? - What does a Jew make? Colloquial for "How are you?" "What are you up to?" The same grammatical construction as the German *Was machst du*? for "How's it going?"

Yiddene

Literally, a Jewish woman; figuratively, a wife

She's such a good *Yiddene*, you'd never know she is a convert.

Chapter Seven

Shtadlans And Shnorrers
The Public Sphere

Life for Jews in Eastern Europe was far from easy. They were often prohibited from owning land, were considered visitors rather than citizens, and could enter only certain professions, commerce and banking among them. It is no surprise then that there were two public arenas in which Jews were active: socialist politics and business.

When they came to the United States, many of the Jewish new immigrants entered business, either as workers in sweatshops or as purveyors of all kinds of goods sold from pushcarts. Those who worked in the sweatshops often were also active in union politics and socialist political movements, so it is not coincidental that Jews, as a demographic group, have tended to vote on the more liberal end of the political spectrum and to be involved with social action projects. Nor is it coincidental that there are many Yiddish words and phrases having to do with politics and business.

I. *Ainer Iz A Ligen, Tzvai Iz Ligens, Drei Iz Politik.* - One Is a Lie, Two Is a Lie, Three Is Politics.

The Russian Tzar and the Austrian Kaiser were the ultimate deciders of the Jews' fate in

Central and Eastern Europe, but it was the petty official that the Jewish community had to deal with on a day-to-day basis. Many political organizations, generally underground ones, sprang up in the Jewish urban centers, and often fought with each other as much as they fought the establishment. Members of the Bund, a secular socialist party dedicated to establishing democratic socialism in Russia, were philosophically and politically in opposition to the Zionists, whom they believed were running away from the problems of the *golus* (Diaspora). The Zionists, who believed they were solving the problems of the *golus* by establishing a Jewish state, were divided into Labor Zionists, Religious Zionists, Revisionist Zionists, Cultural Zionists, and pocketbook Zionists (those who supported the idea of a Jewish state with donations rather than actions). Thus the saying, "Two Jews, three opinions."

Arbeiter Ring
Workman's Circle, a socialist-leaning philanthropic, cultural, political, social, and educational organization that helped immigrant Jews to maintain their ethnic identity while acclimating to American life.

My grandparents were not religious, so they sent my father to the *Arbeiter Ring* to learn about Jewish culture and Yiddish literature instead of to Hebrew School where he would have learned about religious laws and how to pray in Hebrew.

In addition to being involved with union organizing, the Workman's Circle ran (and in some communities, still runs) English language classes for adults, afternoon and summer programs for school children, and credit unions.

The Folksbeine Playhouse, the oldest Yiddish theater still in existence, established in 1915, is run by the Workman's Circle in New York, and offers both classic and modern Yiddish productions.

The I. L. Peretz School network runs almost a dozen community, secular Jewish schools throughout the country, dedicated to keeping alive the culture of the Eastern European Jewish communities. The schools offer language (Hebrew as well as Yiddish), history, song, dance, art, music, and holiday celebrations. The Workman's Circle magazine, Jewish Currents, publishes in English. You can order a Sholem Aleichem bobble head from their website.

Borzhvaz; Borzhvazee
Bourgeois; bourgeoisie; middle class property-owning conformists and capitalists

My grandfather was involved with the Socialist Party and was ashamed when my father bought a house in the suburbs and became a *borzhvaz*.

Farbrent
Literally, burning; refers to someone who is zealous.

My great grandmother was a *farbrente* suffragette.

Freidenker
Freethinker; atheist, secularist

My grandparents almost sat shiva (seven days of mourning following a death) when my aunt announced she would not go to shul any longer because she was a *freidenker* .

Kapore
Scapegoat. Every time there was a problem, the government made the Jews into the *kapore*.

Kemfer
Fighter, activist.

After the Triangle Shirtwaist Factory fire, my great grandfather became a *kemfer* for the unions.

On March 25, 1911, one hundred forty-six mostly young and mainly Jewish immigrant women were killed when fire broke out in the Triangle Shirtwaist Factory. The scraps and piles of fabric burned quickly. On the ninth floor, where most of the victims worked, one exit stairwell quickly filled with smoke, and the other exit door was locked, possibly to prevent theft. The fire escape was inadequate, and the New York City Fire Department ladders were not long enough to reach the upper floors of the ten-floor building. The elevator stopped working, and some of the victims, having pried open the doors, plunged to their deaths down the shaft. Sixty-two of the women, in a scene to be reenacted on September 11, 2001, jumped to their deaths on the pavement below rather than face the flames. It was the worst industrial workplace disaster in New York history for over ninety years.

The workers, some as young as twelve, worked long hours and earned about $7.00 a week. The average age of the victims was nineteen.

Two years before the fire, a massive strike of garment workers known as the Uprising of 20,000, began with a walkout by the workers at the Triangle Shirtwaist Factory. The International Ladies Garment Workers Union (ILGWU) was able to negotiate a collective settlement agreement with many of the other manufacturers, but the owners of the Triangle, Isaac Harris and Max Blanck, refused to sign. They were tried for manslaughter after the fire, but were acquitted. They were later sued in civil court and ordered to pay $75.00 in compensation for each victim.

In the wake of the fire, the ILGWU - and labor unions in general - gained more support for their positions, and were able to push for workplace safety legislation and workman's compensation. The American Society of Safety Engineers was formed just a few months after the fire. The Fire Prevention division of the New York Fire Department was formed by the Factory Commission of 1911, which had been created by the New York legislature in the aftermath of the fire. The Commission was headed by Senator Robert F. Wagner, Alfred E. Smith, and Samuel

Gompers, president of the American Federation of Labor.

The Triangle building now houses the Chemistry Department of New York University, and is on the National Register of Historic Places and was named a National Historic Landmark.

Khaver

Comrade; used in Modern Hebrew for a member of a kibbutz, a pal, or a boyfriend.

He was my great uncle's *khaver* in the union movement.

I was dating an Israeli and when I said I wanted him as a *khaver*, he thought I meant "boyfriend," but I wanted us to be platonic friends.

Khopper

A kidnapper who took the sons of poor Jews to be conscripted into the Russian army for twenty-five years; from the Yiddish word for grabber. Those kidnapped were called cantonistas, referring to the districts (cantons) where their barracks were located.

My great-great grandparents sent my great grandfather to the United States to escape the *khoppers*.

Shokhad

Bribe; payola

When my cousin was on trial for embezzlement, he tried to give a juror a *shokhad*.

My great grandparents tried to get out of Russia by giving the border guard a *shokhad.*

Shtadlan
Court Jew, a factotum who had influence with the rulers and could intercede for the Jewish community. Generally, the *shtadlan* was a banker who lent money to the Christian upper classes.

Sometimes a term of derision for a sell-out, someone who compromised his principles or toadied up to authority.

The *shtadlan* might think the duke is his friend, but the duke hates him even more than he hates the rest of the Jews, because he owes him a lot of money.

II. *Parnosseh Iz A Refueh Tzu Alleh Krenk*
A Good Livelihood Cures All Ills.

Many Jews who sold goods from pushcarts aspired to "move indoors" and open a store. It is, therefore, not unusual that Jews established many of the large department stores, some of which are still in business.

A Quaker from Nantucket named Rowland H. Macy established Macy's in the 1860s. After his death a decade later, the Straus brothers, sons of a German Jewish peddler, purchased the store. (One of the brothers, Isador, later perished on the Titanic along with his wife, who refused to leave the ship without him.)

Among other German Jewish families who founded department stores were the Altmans,

Gimbels, Filenes, Magnins, Kaufmanns, Siegels, Lazaruses, Goldwaters, and Mays.

From the words having to do with commerce, one could get the impression that not only were Jews obsessed by money, but they also used unethical practices in their business dealings, always trying to better the competition, even if they had to resort to underhanded methods to succeed.

A groys gesheft zol er hobn mit shroyre: vus er hot, zol men bei im nit fregn, un vos men fregt zol er nisht hobn. - He should have a large store, and whatever people ask for he should not have, and what he does have should not be requested.

A metzie fon a ganef. - Literally, a bargain from a thief - refers to a good deal, a steal

By the time I used all the discount coupons, my new dress from that luxury story cost so little it was a *metzie fon a ganef.*

Arumgeflikt

Literally, plucked on all sides; figuratively, robbed, swindled

You paid too much for that property. You were arumgeflikt.

Balabost

Literally, "master of the house," used to refer to a boss, the owner of the business. The feminine, *balaboste*, can be the woman who's in charge, but is used more commonly to refer to a housewife, literally, "mistress of the house."

134

My great grandfather worked his way up from a piece worker in a sweat shop to the *balabost* of his own factory.

Women in the fifties would go to college, get married, and stay at home, but they discovered that being a *balaboste* did not earn them a lot of respect.

Bilik
Inexpensive

I don't want to spend a lot of money for a new DVD player. I saw one that was *bilik*, but I wonder if it is any good.

Draikop
Literally, one who turns another's head; a finagler; can also refer to the person who is befuddled.

I went to the appliance store thinking I knew which dishwasher I wanted, and the *draikop* convinced me it was a waste of money and I needed to buy the more expensive model.

By the time he finished with his sales spiel, I was such a *draikop* I had no idea what I was signing.

Er zol altzting zen, un nit hobn mit vos tzu koyfn. - He should see everything, but have nothing to buy it with.

Ganef
A thief.

My former landlord is such a *ganef*. He refused to return our security deposit, even though we cleaned up the apartment.

Ganaivishe shtiklekh
Literally, a piece of thievery; refers to sneaky actions
Be careful doing business with him and his *ganaivishe shtiklekh*.

Gazlan
Robber, swindler.
That *gazlan* tried to charge me double.

Geherik; gehern
Appropriate, to belong
Dos gehert nit tzu dir. - Literally, that does not belong to you; figuratively, that's not your job. It is not your responsibility.

Gelt
Money.
He doesn't care about whether he likes a job. All he cares about is how much gelt he can make.
Oyf drei zakhen shtait di velt: oyf gelt, oyf gelt, oyf gelt. - The world stands on three things: money, money, money.
Tzen shifn mit gold zol er farmorgn, un dos gantze gelt zol er farkrenken. - Ten ships of gold should be his and the money should only make him sick.
Aroysgevorfene gelt

Wasted money, throwing good money after bad.

Buying that stock is *aroysgevorfene gelt.*

Hondel
To haggle, make a deal.
"To Jew someone down" is an anti-Semitic canard for *hondling.*

Kadokhes
Literally, chills and a fever; figuratively, worthless
He thought he'd found a rare stamp, but it was *kadokhes.*

Kapsen
Cheapskate
He is such a *kapsen,* he will not put air conditioning in his factory.

Metzie'ah
A find, a bargain
They bought the house at a great price because the owners needed some quick cash. It was quite a *metzie'ah.*

Mezuma
Cash
I can give you a discount for *mezuma.*

Onsaltn
Literally, to add salt; figuratively, to sweet talk.

Maybe if I try to *onsaltn* her, she'll give me a better deal.

Opgeflikt
Suckered
I was *opgeflikt* into buying flood insurance when I didn't need it.

Opgekrokhshene skhoyre
Shoddy merchandise
I won't shop there. Their *opgekrokhshene skhoyre* is not worth the money.

Oys shidukh
Literally, the engagement is over;
figuratively, "The deal is off!"
When they offered me the job, they said it came with good benefits, but after I accepted their offer, they tried to cut them, so I told them, "*Oys shidukh.*"

Pushka
A box or canister for collecting *tzedaka* (charity)
Every convenience store has a *pushke* for all kinds of charities.

Tzedakah
Charity, is one of the highest values in Jewish life. The Medieval Jewish sage Maimonides listed several levels of *tzedakah*, with the lowest rung being when the donor and

the donee know each other and the highest when both are anonymous.

There's an old Jewish joke about a man who stands up during a fund drive in the synagogue and announces, "I, Moyshe Pupik, of 123 Main Street, owner of Moyshe Pupik's Emporium, purveyor of fine goods, hereby pledge $100,000 - anonymously!

My mother remembers her father lifting her up before the beginning of Shabbos every week so she could put a nickel in the *pushke* hanging from the pantry doorpost. Likely, the *pushke* was the blue and white JNF box.

After the Jewish National Fund was established in 1901, their collection boxes became ubiquitous in Jewish homes and businesses. Its original goal was to purchase land from the Ottoman Empire that controlled Palestine. It also helped fund the first modern Jewish city, Tel Aviv, financed the research and development projects of Jewish scientists, and aided the first kibbutzim. Its major undertaking, one that continues today and is the reason the JNF is well-known to all Jewish school children even now, is reforestation - the planting of trees in Israel. Many a Bar and Bas Mitzvah has trees planted in Israel in their honor.

Shvindl
Sounds like its definition: to swindle, deceive

He tried to shvindl the wrong person, and went to jail.

Chapter Eight

Ess, Ess, Mein Kind
Gastronomical Judaism

Many foods that are considered Jewish - for example, kreplakh, blintzes, borscht, latkes - originated in Eastern European countries. In the U.S., quite a few of these foods have become popular and even mainstream. "kosher-style" or "Jewish" delis, serving so-called "Jewish" foods that are not necessarily kosher (pastrami with cheese, for example) can be found almost everywhere, not just in large cities. Bagels and lox are eaten for breakfast after church services just as often as they are after synagogue services. Bagels have become as ubiquitous as English muffins, and I have seen them served at a Hindu wedding.

Lig in drerd un bak beygl. Lie in the ground and bake bagels! [You can't if you're dead.]

The word kosher generally means foods that conform to Jewish dietary laws, but it literally means "proper, legal," and refers to anything honest and above-board.

Our neighbor is selling DVDs really cheap. I'm not sure they're kosher.

In addition to not eating pork products or shellfish, people who keep kosher do not mix dairy and meat at the same meal. This has led to several categories of foods: *flaishik* (meat); *milchik* (dairy); *pareve* (neutral; also spelled *parve*); *glatt* (from the word for "smooth," refers

141

to unblemished lungs in a cow, and is used colloquially as "super kosher"); *Pesadikh* (kosher for Passover); and, of course, traif (non-kosher food).

Did you ever see the episode of Seinfeld when Kramer deliberately served lobster to Jerry's girlfriend, who kept kosher? What a putz.

I once went to a party with a guy who thought it was funny to tell me the clam dip was made with whitefish. I told all my girlfriends what he did, and even those who didn't keep kosher refused to go out with him.

The most traif sandwich I can think of is ham and cheese with butter on white bread.

Many Yiddish words for these foods are familiar to English-speakers.

Babke
Coffee cake. Not to be confused with bupkis.

The shul keeps serving the same babke every week until it's gone. It's so freezer burned and stale no one will eat it.

Bialy
Similar to a bagel, but minus the hole

My brother prefers a *bialy* to a bagel. He's such a slob that every time he eats a bagel, the cream cheese oozes out of the hole onto his shirt. There's no hole in a *bialy*, so his shirt stays clean, until he spills coffee on it.

The word bagel comes from the Middle High German word *broug*, a ring or bracelet. It likely originated in the Polish town of Krakow. The word *bialy*, which is short for *bialystoker kuchen* (Bialystok's Cake), comes from the name of the Polish town of Bialystok.

Blintz

An Eastern European version of a crepe, usually filled with farmer's cheese, blueberries, cherries, or apples, and served with either sour cream or apple sauce.

She's such a snob that she calls her blintzes crepes.

Borscht

A soup made with beets and served hot or cold with a dollop of sour cream or a piece of boiled potato. It was a popular enough dish to have given its name to the Borscht Belt, the Jewish resort section of the Catskills where many comedians got their start, often as waiters. Not to be confused with shav (made with sorrel) or gazpacho (different ethnicity).

Hey, klutz! Careful you don't spill the borscht. You'll never get the stains out.

Bronfn
Whiskey

Odem yesode meofe vesofe leofe - beyno-lveyno iz gut a trink bronfn. - A man comes from the dust and in the dust he will end - in the meantime it is good to drink whiskey.

In an example of names being based on occupations, the Bronfman family of Canada, leading Jewish philanthropists, made its fortune through the liquor distillery Seagram's.

Challah

The egg bread, often braided, used to celebrate the Sabbath.

They almost got a divorce over their argument about whether challah should be sliced thin or thick for French toast.

Ess nisht di challah far a moytze. - Don't eat the challah before you have made the blessing. In other words, don't have sex before marriage. (In English, we say, "Why buy the cow when the milk is for free?")

Ess

Eat. Usually used as an exhortation as in the oft heard *Ess, ess, mein kind* (Eat, eat, my child.)

You're too skinny. *Ess*.

Ess, ess, mein kind. There are children starving it [fill in the blank].

There's an old pun about a Jewish cruise ship, the *Ess, Ess, Mein Kind.*

Farfel

Broken up pieces of matzo.

He's so dumb he thought I was talking about Shari Lewis' puppet when I said I needed to pick up some *farfel*.

Get your hearing checked. I said "*farfel*," not falafel!

Flanken

A cut of meat from short ribs, usually boiled or stewed.

In my opinion, flanken is one of the reasons many people think "Jewish haute cuisine" is an oxymoron.

Fliegl
Wing

My grandmother always put the *fliegl* in the chicken soup pot. Buffalo wings were unknown in the shtetl!

Forshpeis
An appetizer.

When they come to our house for dinner, we serve a full-course meal, but when they invite for dinner, all they serve is a *forshpeis*.

Fress; fresser
Not just to eat, but to be a glutton.

You better get to the buffet table before my cousin does. He's such a *fresser*, there won't be anything left for the rest of us.

Er frest vi a ferd. - He eats like a horse.

Gedempte fleish
Pot roast, brisket

I don't like *gedempte fleish*. It's always overdone.

Gefilt croyt; holeptzes; holishkes; prokas
Stuffed cabbage; the names change depending on the country of origin.

My assimilated mother did not make *holishkes* or *prokas*, but stuffed cabbage.

Gefilte fish
Literally, stuffed fish. When made from scratch, similar to meat balls, but with ground up carp, pike, or other white fish mixed with eggs (as a binder) and matzo meal or flour. Originally, the ground up fish was stuffed back into the fish skin (thus, the name), but now is generally served as individual balls (usually from a jar) or baked in a loaf. It is always served with horseradish.

My goyishe neighbor loved the appetizer I served until she found out it was gefilte fish. She barely made it to the bathroom before she threw up.

Geshmakt
Delicious, tasty
He told me gorgonzola cheese is quite *geshmakt*, but I can't stand the smell.

Gogl-mogl
Originally, an egg-based homemade dessert from Russia and popular in Central and Eastern Europe, as well as in Caucasus. Also refers to a drink made from honey, warm milk, raw egg, and brandy or other hard liquor.

Whenever I had a sore throat, my grandmother would make me a *gogl-mogl*. It always made me feel sicker.

Gribenes
Crispy chicken skin; cracklings, usually fried with shmaltz and onions.

My cardiologist would have a fit if she knew I still eat *gribenes*.

Kasha
Buckwheat groats, a whole grain that is healthful if made with olive or other vegetable oil and not in the traditional way with shmaltz.

He gave me one of those pillows stuffed with buckwheat. It's so uncomfortable I wanted to open it up and cook the contents with *varnishkes* (bowtie pasta).

Khalushes
Disgusting, nauseating

I'm glad squid isn't kosher. I think it sounds *khalushes*.

Khrain
Horseradish

He made his own *khrain* only once, but the shlimazel forgot to open a window and almost wound up in the hospital.

A bilingual pun: There was once a shortage of horseradish. The only country that had any was Spain. An airlift was arranged to send the horseradish to other countries. The press release announced, "The khrain in Spain is mainly on the plane."

Kikhel
A crispy, concave, puffy, pastry coated with sugar

It sounds like a weird combination, but chopped herring is great on kikhel.

Kishke
Stuffed derma.

I served him *kishke* but didn't tell him what it was until after he'd finished it and asked for more. He still hasn't forgiven me.

Kishke is made from intestine casings filled with meat, flour, breading, and spices. It's not as disgusting as it sounds - in fact, it's delicious - and, unlike haggis, is baked not boiled.

K'naidlakh
Matzo balls

The first time she made *k'naidlakh*, they came out like canon balls. Her *makhatonista* has never let her forget it.

K'nobl
Garlic

It's traditional to eat *k'nobl* on Friday nights, because it's supposed to be an aphrodisiac. [It's a mitzvah for married couples to have sex on Shabbos.]

Kremzel

Fried potato pancake

We tried to explain to the kids that chocolate chips and whipped cream didn't go well on top of *kremzel*.

A *kremzel* is similar to a latke, but because it is made without flour as a binder, it can be - and usually is - served for Passover not Chanukah.

Kreplakh

A filled pastry, the Jewish version of wontons or ravioli.

Vilst essn bei mir kreplakh? - Do you want to eat kreplakh with me? Said as a threat, similar to the English, "Are you looking for a knuckle sandwich?"

Kugel

A baked pudding, made with noodles or matzo, mixed with eggs and either onions and/or other chopped vegetables, or with cheese, apples, raisins, and/or other fruit.

Az men esst Shabbos kugel, iz men di gantzeh vokh zat. - Eat kugel on the Sabbath and be full all week.

Galitzianers (Jews from Ukraine and Poland) prefer their kugel sweet, while Litvaks (Jews from Lithuania and environs) prefer it savory. One explanation is that apples and honey were more plentiful in the south where the Galitzianers lived, while Litvaks further north were able to get onions and salt more easily.

Latke

A potato pancake. Served with sour cream or applesauce.

She's such a phony. She served store-bought frozen latkes and tried to pass them off as homemade.

Lekekh

Honey or sponge cake

She's the only one I know whose *lekekh* is either flat or not sweet enough.

Lokhshn

Noodles

He's got *lokhshn* for brains.

I prefer *lokshn* kugel to potato kugel.

Lox

Smoked salmon; Jewish sushi. Usually served on top of bagels with cream cheese.

You can dress it up all you want with capers and roe and fancy crackers, but it's still lox.

The etymology of the word, which means "salmon" in Yiddish, goes back to the Proto-Indo-European word for fish, laks. Cognates (lax, lakhs, laszisza, losos) can be found in many Teutonic, Scandinavian, and Eastern European languages.

Mamaliga

Corn meal porridge; the Eastern European version of polenta.

I don't care how good it's supposed to taste, to me *mamaliga* is not *geshmakt*.

Mandelbrot; kamishbrot

Literally, almond bread; similar to twice-baked biscotti. *Kamishbrot* is the Ukrainian version of the same cookie.

I can't believe you'd spend $3.00 at a fancy coffee place for the same *mandelbrot* my grandmother used to make.

Matzo

The unleavened bread eaten at Passover.

I've found an inexpensive cure for diarrhea: eat enough matzo and you won't shit for a month.

Meichel

A treat

When some women want a *meichel*, they buy shoes. I treat myself to an ice cream sundae.

Nosh; nosherei

To snack, nibble between meals.

She can't figure out why she can't lose weight, but all she does is nosh on junk food all day.

Nosherei is what you snack on, and often means junk food. Nosherei is similar to khazerei, which comes from the Hebrew word for pig, and always means junk food.

A nosher and a *khazer* are slightly different, too. A nosher is someone who eats between meals, who "grazes," but a *khazer* stuffs his mouth full of food while noshing.

Examples:

Stop eating that *nosherei*, you'll ruin your appetite for supper.

Have an apple instead of that *khazerei*. It's better for you.

Nusl
Nuts

He always brings *nusl* to our house when we invite him for dinner. He hasn't noticed yet that we never serve them.

Von zup zu nuslakh. - From soup to little nuts.

Peklflaish
Corned beef

Hot *peklflaish* on rye bread with mustard is a real *meichel*. But serving it on white bread with mayo is a *shande*.

P'tcha
Jellied calves feet

He almost threw up when they served him *p'tcha*, which they consider a delicacy.

Rugelakh and Shnecken

Small, sweet, rolled, crescent or snail shaped pastries filled with a variety of spreads, fruits, nuts, cinnamon. Shnecken (usually spelled schnecken) is of German origin and is made with yeast. Rugelakh (rugelach) often has cream cheese added to the batter. Schnecke means "snail" in German, and rogale is a horn-shaped pastry in Poland, so what you call these sweet rolls depends on your family's origin.

My German-born grandmother always made shnecken and my Polish-born one made rugelakh. No matter the name, they were delicious.

Shmaltz

Fat, particularly chicken fat; as an adjective, the word shmaltzy refers to anything overly sentimental.

I can't stand those shmaltzy shows on TV at Christmas time.

Shmaltz was used to fry almost anything that could be fried. It has gone the way of other delicacies like gribenes (crispy chicken skin) and liver with onions.

The advent of Crisco shortening was a major cause of rejoicing in many a kosher kitchen, since shmaltz was by its nature flaishik (meat) and could not be used in the preparation of dairy meals. Crisco, being made from vegetables, was parve (neutral) and could be used to fry any foods, and was used for baking parve pastries. It revolutionized kosher cuisine.

Shmear

Sounds like "smear," which is what it is. It's what you put on your bagel when you want only a bit of cream cheese.

I'll take a poppy seed and a shmear.

Can also be used to refer to a bribe.

I'll shmear the ticket seller and get us better seats.

Shnaps
Generic term for liquor.
Who said Jews don't drink hard liquor? After services every day, the men used to get together for a shtikl herring and some shnaps.

Shmek'n
To smell
There's nothing like the *shmek* of frying onions and garlic.
A fremdeh bissen shmekt zis. - Another's tidbit smells sweet. ["The grass is always greener."]

Shpritz
Literally, spray. Usually refers to seltzer. When served by itself (instead of as a mixer), it's called "two cents plain."
Don't get too close to him - when he talks, he shpritzes.

Smeteneh
Sour cream
She was so *farshimlt* she used *smeteneh* instead of whipped cream on top of the ice cream sundaes

Taam;batampt
Taste, from the Hebrew word for taste, *ta'am*.

154

This brand of soup has no *taam*. It needs some *k'nobl*.

She thinks her turkey is *batampt*, but it's always too dry.

There is a brand of kosher condiments (pickles, sauerkraut) called *BaTempte*.

Oystaam

No taste; can refer either to flavor or to a sense of style.

She thinks she's such a good cook, but her food is *oystaam*.

There was a time when wearing white shoes after Labor Day was *oystaam*.

Umbatampt

Tasteless

No one has the heart to tell him that his hamburgers are *umbatampt*.

Taiglakh

Small pieces of dough covered in honey.

I tried to make *taiglakh* like my grandmother did at Rosh Hashanah, so we'd have a sweet year. But mine are more like a disastrous year.

Tzimmes

A casserole usually made with carrots and prunes, but also can be made with sweet potatoes or other vegetables or fruits. It refers also to overreacting to a troublesome or messy situation.

It's no big deal. I don't know why you have to make such a *tzimmes* out of it.

Zoyere ugerke

Literally, sour cucumber; pickle (The word gherkin is from the Slavic word for cucumber.)

You can't get a *zoyere ugerke* that's *batampt* from a jar. You have to buy it from a barrel.

Zup

Soup

Chicken zup might not cure the common cold, but it makes it more bearable.

Nothing - celebrations, holidays, shiva, and even fast days - takes place in Judaism without food, and every Jewish holiday has its own traditional foods associated with it.

Shabbos (Sabbath): Challah, gefillte fish, chicken for Friday night. On Saturday, it was traditional to have *cholent*, a dense stew made of beans, potatoes, other root vegetables, and meat and slow cooked on a low heat. Because observant Jews do not initiate the use of fire or electricity on Shabbos, they do not cook from scratch from sundown Friday until sundown Saturday. Cholent could be prepared before the beginning of Shabbos and left on the stove on a blekh (a warming tray) over a low flame - or, nowadays, in a crockpot.

Rosh Hashanah (New Year): A round challah, to represent the continuous cycle of the year. Honey, to dip apples or challah into, or baked into a honey cake, for a sweet year.

Yom Kippur (Day of Atonement): A fast day, but it is customary to have a light, non-spicy, easily digested meal before the holiday, and to break the fast with another light meal.

Sukkos (Festival of Booths): Any food with a mixture of ingredients, to symbolize abundance. (It is widely believed that the Pilgrims based Thanksgiving on this harvest festival.) Stuffed cabbage is a traditional meal. Pomegranates are also symbolic on this holiday, as tradition holds that the pomegranate contains six hundred thirteen seeds, which is the number of mitzvos, commandments, a Jew is obligated to observe.

Chanukah: To commemorate the miracle of the one-day supply of oil that lasted for eight days, any food fried in oil is eaten. Potato latkes are the most common of these foods, although in Israel *sufganyot*, jelly donuts, are popular.

Purim: To celebrate Queen Esther's successful intervention against Haman, who wanted to destroy the Jews, hamantashen, a triangular pastry filled with pureed fruit such as cherries, blueberries, apricots, prunes or *lekhvar* (poppy seeds) are distributed to friends. The word translates as Haman's pocket, and is supposed to look like his three-cornered hat.

Tu B'shvat (The fifteenth of the month of *Shevat*): A minor holiday, *Tu B'shvat* is the Jewish Arbor Day. It falls in the late winter or early spring, when the almond trees begin to bloom in Israel. Recently, it has become a Jewish version of Earth Day. The traditional foods are nuts and dried fruits - in other words, trail mix - or *bakhser*, carob, also known as Locust bean or St. John's bread (but not among Jews).

Pesakh (Passover): The entire holiday revolves around food, as there are additional dietary laws that forbid any leavening agents. The Israelites left Egypt so quickly that their bread did not have time to rise, so Jews still eat only unleavened bread - matzo - for the week of the holiday. The restriction applies to all foods with leavening, and matzo meal and potato starch are used in place of wheat flour. Traditional foods include matzo brei, pieces of matzo mixed with eggs and fried, a Passover version of French toast.

Shavuos (Festival of Weeks): Coming exactly seven weeks after *Pesakh*, *Shavuos* is a spring harvest holiday, with dairy foods being traditional. Blintzes, filled with cheese, blueberries, or cherries, and topped with either sour cream or apple sauce, are the traditional food for the holiday.

Chapter Nine

Frailikh Zol Zein
It's A Good Life

Times may have been difficult for Jews in Eastern Europe, but they still knew how to celebrate a *simkha* (a happy event). And anything could qualify as a *simkha*, especially life cycle events.

There are rituals for every stage of a person's life, each event followed by a *seudas mitzvah*, a festive meal to mark the fulfillment of the obligation. A baby is welcomed into the world by remembering the covenant God made with the Israelites through the *bris milah* (circumcision) for a boy and a naming ceremony for a girl. When children begin to learn to read, they are given wooden cutouts of the *alef-bais* (alphabet) coated with honey, so they'll associate education with sweetness. The coming of age is marked by the Bar or Bas Mitzvah ceremony - and party. Weddings are so joyous they are traditionally divided into three parts: the engagement, the signing of the *kesubah* (contract), and the formal ceremony in front of witnesses and under the *khuppah* (canopy). (Today, most couples combine the three ritual elements into one ceremony.) Weddings are considered so important that they are held (although without the music and dancing) even if the family is still in mourning. And even death is marked by traditional foods: eggs to

159

symbolize the cycle of life and renewal, pastries and candies to sweeten the mourners' lives.

Joyousness and celebration also marked holidays: Shabbos isn't complete without singing and dancing (albeit a capella, as it's forbidden to use musical instruments on the Sabbath). Purim is so much fun that the entire month is dedicated to frivolity: "Be happy, it's *Adar*" is the preferred greeting during the month. We are commanded on Purim to become so drunk that we no longer know the difference between "Blessed be Mordecai" and "Cursed be Haman." It's also the only time that the Biblical prohibition against cross-dressing is lifted, with costumes an integral part of the celebration.

So be *frailikh* and use some of the following words.

Barukh Hashem.
Thank God
Barukh Hashem. - It could have been worse.
How are things going? *Barukh Hashem*, going well.

Bis hundert un tzvantzik yor.
Until a hundred and twenty years.
Moses lived to the age of one hundred-and-twenty, so the expression is a traditional blessing on birthdays and anniversaries.

Mazel tov on your fiftieth birthday. May you live *bis hundert un tzvantzik yor*!

If I can't eat shmaltz, I don't want to live *bis hundert un tzvantzik yor*.

Glick

Luck

Just my *glick* - I found the perfect dress for the wedding in the first store I went to, and then found out my sister had bought the same one.

Himmel

Heaven, sky.

Gott im Himmel, did you see that guy run the red light?

Laiben ahf dein kop!

Life on your head; Good job! Nice work! Can be sardonic.

You mixed up the *milchik* and *flaishik* utensils. *Laiben ahf dein kop*!

Mekhei'ya

A reviver; a relief

I love my sister, but she can talk on and on about nothing. It's a real *mekhei'ya* when she finally shuts up.

After that heat outside, the air conditioning is a real *mekhei'ya*.

Nakhas; Shep Nakhas

Pride; to take pride in

They're the kind of grandparents who *shep nakhas* if their grandchildren don't flunk any courses.

Nisht geferlakh

No big deal

Don't worry about spilling the soup. The table cloth can go into the washing machine. *Nisht geferlakh.*

Olam Ha'ba

The world to come; can be the afterlife or the Messianic age.

My elderly neighbor plans to see her late husband again in *Olam Ha'ba.*

Nations will finally learn to get along - in *Olam Ha'ba.*

The question of whether Jews believe in Heaven and Hell can best be summed up by two words: "It depends." (Another oft heard two-word answer is: "Who knows?") Jews have an ambivalent and rather undefined view of the afterlife. Resurrection is a central tenet of traditional belief, occurring when the Messiah comes, which is one of the reasons Jews do not cremate bodies. . (The practice has become more frequent among non-traditional Jews in the United States. But many who do not believe in resurrection still do not favor cremation, because of the Holocaust, when Jewish bodies were burned not out of respect but because they were considered trash.) The Talmud refers to the *gilgul neshomos*, the revolution of souls, which the Zohar, the central text of Kabala and Jewish mysticism, interprets as reincarnation.

Generally, however, the Jewish texts do not have much to say about an afterlife. For this reason, Judaism is considered an "earth-bound" religion, one that focuses more on our actions here rather than worrying about what will happen after.

Pahst
Appropriate

It was a difficult situation to be in, but his behavior was *pahst*.

Oyf der shukh pahst, kenst im trogen. - If the shoe fits, wear it.

Shekhekheyanu

Literally, "Who has kept us alive," it is the first word of a prayer of thanks recited whenever there is a happy or special occasion or at the beginning of a new endeavor. The prayer blesses God "who has kept us alive, sustained us, and brought us to this time.

After three tries, he finally got his driver's license. He should say a *Shekhekheyanu*.

Yasher koyekh

Congratulations, good job; can be ironic.

After spending hundreds of dollars on lottery tickets, you finally won a few bucks? *Yasher koyekh*!

I.Compliments and Terms of Endearment

Saikhel

Common sense, brains, smarts; can be a compliment or a term of derision when used sarcastically.

She realized she was being followed on a deserted road, and there was no cell phone reception, so she used her *saikhel*, drove to the closest convenience store, and leaned on her horn. The cops caught the guy several miles away - he was still speeding away.

You can't wear sandals in the snow! Use some *saikhel*!

Ain mol a saikhel, dos tzvaiteh mol khain, dem dritten mol gil men in di tzain. - The first time it's smart, the second time it's cute, the third time you get a sock in the teeth.

A kindershe saikhel iz oykhet a saikhel. - A child's wisdom is also wisdom.

Es felt em der saikhel heioshor. - He has no common sense.

Shtarker

Someone who is strong, physically or emotionally. Can also refer to a bodyguard, bouncer, enforcer.

Don't try to be a *shtarker* and move that piano yourself. Get some help.

After his wife died, he had to be a *shtarker* for the children.

The *shtarkers* surrounding that rock star were scary looking.

Tzaddik

A righteous person

If we had saints in Judaism, that *tzaddik* would be one.

A tzaddik vos vais er iz a tzaddik iz kain tzaddik nit. - A righteous man who knows he is righteous is not.

Tzutzik
An ambitious or energetic person

I get tired just thinking about everything that *tzutzik* does all the time.

Zieskeit
Sweetie

That baby is such a *zieskeit*. Too bad she'll become a teenager some day.

II. Celebrations

Badkhan
Entertainer; jester

In the movie *The Wedding Singer*, Adam Sandler's character was a *badkhan*.

A badkhan makht alle menschen frailikh un alain ligt er in drerd. - A jester makes everyone laugh and he alone is miserable.

Bar Mitzvah
The coming-of-age ritual for a boy.

His Bar Mitzvah reception was more about the bar (as in free drinks) than the mitzvah (good deeds).

The two-word phrase Bar Mitzvah literally means "son of the obligation," and indicates a boy who is thirteen and has attained the legal status of an adult. The responsibility for keeping Jewish traditions and rituals now passes from his parents to him. The phrase has come to refer to the service at which the boy is first counted in the minyan (quorum of ten adults for a public prayer service). At that time, he is called to the bimah (literally, stage) to recite the blessings before the reading of the Torah scroll, and sometimes to read from the Torah and Haftara (commentary). These days it also means the party marking the occasion. Once a boy turns thirteen, however, he is a Bar Mitzvah and has the legal status of an adult even without the ritual or the party.

Bas Mitzvah
The coming-of-age ritual for a girl.
I've been to weddings less lavish than her Bas Mitzvah party.

The word *bas* is the Ashkenazi pronunciation of the Hebrew word *bat*, which means "daughter," and a Bas Mitzvah is a twelve-year-old girl who is now of legal age and could marry. There was no formal ceremony to mark the occasion until March 18, 1922, when Rabbi Mordecai M. Kaplan, the founder of Reconstructionist Judaism, developed a synagogue ritual for his oldest daughter, Judith. In these days of equal rights, rites, and responsibilities for girls and women, the Bas Mitzvah ceremony is indistinguishable from the Bar Mitzvah one, and is also held at the age of thirteen. In more traditional synagogues, the age is still twelve and the girl is called to the bimah on Friday night, when the Torah scroll is not removed from the aron kodesh, the holy ark.

Draidel

A spinning top, used in a gambling game at Chanukah.

That kid is so hyper he looks like a draidel that never stops spinning.

The word draidel comes from *drai*, the Yiddish word for turn or twist. The game is played for gelt (money), either real coins or chocolate ones, called Chanukah gelt*. Each side is labeled with a Hebrew letter: *Nun*, for *nes* (miracle); *gimmel*, for *gadol* (great); *hai*, for *haya* (was); *shin*, for *sham* (there). The resultant sentence means, "A great miracle happened there," referring to the apocryphal story of the one-day's supply of consecrated oil for the Temple that lasted the eight days. (In Israel, the final letter is *pai* for the word *po*, "here," so the sentence is, "A great miracle happened here.") Depending on which letter is showing when the top stops spinning, the player gets nothing (nun), all (gimmel), half (hai), or has to add to the pot (shin).

*Shameless self promotion: Check out the cozy mystery *Chanukah Guilt* (no it's not a typo; it's a pun), written by this author. And for more about Chanukah, go to:
https://whyninecandles.com, also by this author.

Farbrengen
A party or gathering, especially religious or family

We went to a *farbrengen* last weekend. There was just as much dancing as there was study.

Farpitzed
Dressed up
Aren't you a bit *farpitzed* to go to a movie?

Farshnoshked
Drunk
I could not believe how strong that Cosmopolitan was - after one, I was completely *farshnoshked*.

Fartootzed
Overdressed, overdone
She always comes to work all *fartootzed*, but most of us just wear jeans.

Kapelye
Musical band
I hate going to a party that has a DJ. The music is too loud and the DJ's are always so shmultzy. So we decided to have a *kapelye* instead.

The iconic Jewish song *Hava Nagillah* is Hebrew, not Yiddish. And it's not an ancient traditional song either. The tune is of Chasidic origin, but the lyrics, which are attributed to Abraham Zevi Idelsohn, may actually have been written by his student, Moshe Nathanson - who was twelve years old when his teacher gave him the task of coming up with lyrics to the wordless melody in 1907.

Kumsitz

Literally, come sit; figuratively, a sing-a-long, often around a campfire; similar to a hootenany.

The youth group tried to end every meeting with a *kumsitz*, but most of the kids would sneak off for a smoke.

Ongepatchkt

Overdressed, overdone

She looks so *ongepatchkt* with all that makeup on.

I have never seen a house with so many tchotchkes. It's really *ongepatchkt*.

Tummler

Entertainer, slapstick comic, from the Yiddish word for noise, *tummel* .

A lot of standup comics got their training as *tummlers* in the Borscht Belt.

He thinks he's a dramatic actor, but he's just a *tummler*.

III. Weddings

A wedding is one of the most important and joyful rites in Judaism. Even if someone has died and the family is still in the period of mourning, an already scheduled wedding still takes place (but without the music and entertainment). One of the first blessings given a newborn, when it is formally given its name, is "May s/he grow into a life of Torah, *khuppah, oo'ma'asim tovim* - Torah (learning), the bridal canopy (marriage, or family devotion), and good deeds."

A khissoren, di kalleh iz tzu shain. To a fault-finder, even the bride is too pretty.

Alte moyd
Old maid
In some traditional communities, an unmarried girl of eighteen is already an *alte moyd*.

Alter bokher
Bachelor
My uncle is an *alter bokher*. My mother thinks he's a *faigele*, but I think he's just afraid of commitment.

Aufruf
Literally, calling up. It refers to the Torah honor given to a groom (and nowadays to the bride, too) on the Shabbos before the wedding.
The *aufruf* was an embarrassment. The *khoson* didn't know the blessings.

Besulah
A legal status in the *kesuba* referring to a woman who has never been married. (The other

two categories are a widow or a divorced woman.) Her marital status determined the amount of the bride price the groom had to pay. The highest amount was for a besiulah.

She may have been a *besulah*, but she was no virgin.

Christians interpet Isaiah 7:14 as referring to the virgin birth. The prophet used *alma*, a synonym for *besulah*. Both words can be used to refer to a "young maiden" or "unmarried woman," although the primary meaning of *alma* is "virgin." The words "never married woman" and "virgin" became interchangeable because of the assumption that a woman who had never been married was a virgin. As many "six-month pregnancies" demonstrate, it's an erroneous assumption.

Kallah
Bride
She was the exception to the rule that every *kallah* is beautiful on her wedding day.

Kesuba
Marriage contract, from the Hebrew word for something written.
Instead of using a preprinted *kesuba*, they had one custom illustrated by a professional calligrapher. The problem is, he spelled the kallah's name wrong.

Khasana
Wedding

She started planning her daughter's *khasana* before she was born!

Khoson
Groom
I have never see a *khoson* as nervous as he was.

Khuppah
Wedding canopy
They decorated the *khuppah* with roses, and the maid of honor had an allergy attack on the *bima*.

Nokh di khuppah iz shpet di kharoteh. - after the khuppah, it's too late for regrets.

Makhatonim
Child's in-laws
Their *makhatonim* didn't help out financially with the wedding, but still insisted on criticizing everything.

Makhatonista
Mother-in-law
My sister's *makhatonista* is the model for every mother-in-law joke.

Makhotin
Father-in-law
He got along better with his *makhotin* than he did with his own father.

Shadkhan
Matchmaker

His mother was getting so worried she'd never have grandchildren she secretly hired a *shadkhan* for her son.

After all those years of blind dates, singles bars, and online dating sites, she was beginning to think a *shadkhan* might be a good idea.

A bokher a shadkhan, a moyd a bubbe konnen nisht zein. A bachelor a matchmaker, a spinster a grandmother - these cannot be.

A shadkhan must zein a ligner. A matchmaker must be a liar.

Bei a shadkhan iz nit kain meese kallah. - According to a *shadkhan*, there's no homely bride.

Shidukh
Arranged marriage
I threatened my daughter that if she doesn't meet someone soon, I'll find someone and make a *shidukh* between them.

Yikhes
Lineage, family connections; someone who has *yikhes* is a *yakhsen*.

He's a nogoodnik, but still managed to marry into a family with a lot of *yikhes*.

Even though he had no employment history, he got a good job because of he's a *yakhsen*.

Chapter Ten

Altzding Lozst Zikh Oys Mit A Gevain
When Things Go Bad

Often, the difficulties and tragedies of Eastern European Jewish life far outweighed the joyous occasions. One of the most often heard expressions was *Shver zu zein a Yid* - "It's hard to be a Jew." Jews were often denied citizenship in the countries in which they lived, even if they had been there for centuries. Often forbidden to own land, their choices of occupations were limited. Money lending was allowed, as it was considered usury and forbidden to Christians. (Yiddish was useful for commerce, as Jews from different countries in Europe were able to converse with each other.) It wasn't only the Jews' livelihoods but life itself that was precarious. They could not move freely from place to place or live anywhere they wanted. Expulsions were a fact of life, dating from Roman times to the Inquistion to Shakespeare's England, and continuing into the Twentieth Century. Persecution, blood libels, pogroms, rape were expected. (Although matrilineal descent, meaning that a child's status as a Jew is determined through the mother's rather than the father's religion, has its roots in Biblical times, many believe it is so the child conceived through the rape of a Jewish woman by a non-Jew during a pogrom would still be Jewish.) And there are many Jewish fast days throughout the year that commemorate catastrophes that befell the

Jewish people, from the destruction of both Temples in Jerusalem, the First by the Babylonians in 586 BCE and the Second by the Romans in 70 CE, to the more recent additions of Holocaust Memorial Day and Israel's Memorial Day for fallen soldiers. It is not suprising that there are so many Yiddish words for bad luck.

I. Misfortune

Auf tzolokes
Bad luck
He got brand new tires and, *ahf tzolokes*, drove over some broken glass in the middle of the street two days later.

Altzding lozst zikh oys mit a gevain.
Everything ends in weeping.
Don't celebrate your new job until you sign the contract. *Altzding lozst zikh oys mit a gevain.*

Az okh un vai
Tough luck
He just moved into a new house, and then got downsized. *Az okh un vai.*

Balagan
A noisy tumult, a mess
I made the mistake of going to my *ainikl's* third birthday party at an indoor amusement park. What a *balagan*! How can so few kids make so much noise?

The first time I tried to make *hamantashen* at home, the bag of flour broke all over the floor. What a *balagan*!

Farfallen
Doomed; predetermined bad luck
It is *farfallen* that as soon as I put on a new pair of panty hose, I get a run in them.

Fintzter un glitshik
Literally, dark and slippery; figuratively, miserable
It's been a *fintzter un glitshik* winter. I can't wait for spring.

Gehakhte tzoris
Literally, chopped up; figuratively, terrible trouble
I've had such *gehakhte tzoris* lately. Nothing is going right.

Geshrei
Yell, shout
He gave such a *geshrei* when he stubbed his toe; I thought he'd cut it off!

Nit gut
Not good
Oy, the situation in the Middle East is *nit gut. Nit gut.*

Shvakh
Weak

He planned to sue his former boss for age discrimination, but then realized his case was *shvakh* - the guy they hired to replace him is older than he is.

Tzoris/Auf tzoris
Trouble, in serious trouble

I can't believe how much *tzoris* they're having selling their house.

If they can't sell the house soon, they'll be *ahf tzoris*.

Umglik
Misfortune, literally "unluck."

It was their *umglik* to buy a house when it was a seller's market, and to have to sell it in a buyer's market.

Eyn umglik iz far im vainik. - One misfortune is too few for him.

Umglik binds tzunoyf. - Misfortune binds together. (Misery loves company.)

Vern a tel
To be ruined; in shambles

I spilled grape juice all over my new sweater. *Vern a tel* if I don't soak it right away in cold water.

A *tel* in Hebrew is the word for a hill or mound, and often it covers an archaeological site. Tel Aviv, for example, is Hebrew for Hill of Spring.

II. Abuse -Physical and Osychologocal

Frosk
Slap
When was the last time a girl gave a boy a *frosk* on the cheek for trying to kiss her?

Khoyzek; khoyzek makhn
Ridicule; Make fun of
I was only *khoyzek makhn* about how he looks in shorts, but he got insulted. He can't take a joke.

Kitzel
Tickle
Since when is a *kitzel* child abuse?

Klap
Hit
He got me so mad I wanted to give him a *klap*.
A klap fargait, a vort bashtait. - A blow passes, a word lingers.

Mekhieleh
Forgiveness, pardon, but often used ironically or euphemistically.
Mekhiela? I can't possibly forgive you for embarrassing me in public!
Vilst a kopeh in mekhieleh arein? - Do you want a kick in the pardon-the-expression?

Potch

Tap, slap

That yenta next door accused me of spanking my son. All I did was give him a *potch en tuchus*.

In my day, if a boy tried to kiss a girl on the first date, he got a *potch en punim*.

Shmeis

Thrash; can be used metaphorically for a rousing defeat in a game.

All the sports mavens predicted the Red Sox would *shmeis* the Yankees, but the Yankees got a winning homer in extra innings.

Strashn

To threaten

I know it's bad parenting to *strashn* and not follow through, but it's hard to break the pattern.

Tshepn

To pick on

Don't *tshep* your little sister. You're being a bully.

Zetz

Jab, poke; can be verbal as well as physical

He gave me a *zetz*, but I didn't think of a comeback until later that night. I wish I could think more quickly on my feet

III. Confusion

Yiddish-speakers must have often been perplexed, as there are many synonyms for the condition.

Farblonget
Lost, confused
I am so *farblonget*, I have no idea if I added the sugar to the cake mix yet.

Fardrimmeled
Dreaming, daydreaming
I must have been *fardrimmeled* while coming home from work tonight - I drove right past my street.

Farklempt
Unpleasantly surprised, distraught, choked up, extremely emotional
When my neighbor discovered her winning lotto ticket was just a gag gift from her husband, she was quite *farklempt* and made him sleep on the couch that night.
Farklempt comes from *klempn*, the Yiddish word for "tug," and was popularized by Mike Myers' Saturday Night Live character Linda Richman, a suburban Jewish matron talk show host. When using the word, Myers would fan his face and pat his chest, as though the character was having heart palpitations (or a hot flash).

Farmished
Mixed up, messed up
I am usually pretty good at figuring out how to use a database program, but this one has me *farmished*.

Farmutshet
Tired out
I am so *farmutshet* I can't think straight.

Farpatshket
Messed up
You'll have to explain what happened again. I'm really *farpatshket*.

Fartshadet
Distracted
I was so *fartshadet* at the staff meeting today, I didn't absorb a thing my supervisor said.

IV. How to Use "Oy"

The interjection oy is commonly used as a response to bad news. In combination with other words, it takes on various degrees of seriousness:

Oy
Oh.
Statement: I got a flat tire. Response: Oy.
Oy vai. Oh, no.
Statement: I had a fender-bender. Response: Oy vai.
Oy vai iz mir. - Oh, woe is me.

Statement: I went through a red light and broadsided another car. Response: *Oy vai iz mir*.

Oy gevalt. Oh, alas.

Statement: The car was stolen. Response: *Oy gevalt*.

Oy, Gottenyu Oh, my God.

Statement: The car was totaled. Response: *Oy, gottenu*.

Four Jews are sitting in a restaurant. For a long time, nobody says a word. Finally, one groans, "Oy."

"Oy vey," says the second.

"Nu," sighs the third.

At this, the fourth gets up and says, "Listen, if you don't stop talking politics, I'm leaving."

V. Other Expressions of Woe

When things are so bad it's not enough to say oy, try some of these words:

Genug iz genug
Enough is enough; often said in frustration, mostly by parents of toddlers or teenagers.

It is just been one thing after another. *Genug iz genug already*.

I told you before to turn down that CD player! It is giving me a headache. *Genug iz genug!*

Gehenem
Hell. If many Jews find it comforting to believe in *Olam Ha'ba*, they prefer not to believe

in *Gehenem*. The word is not used as a curse (*dred* - ground - serves that purpose), but as a place name.

I hate my job. It is like being in *Gehenem*.

Gornisht helfen.
Nothing helps.

My friend convinced her husband to finally take Viagra, but unfortunately *gornisht helfen*.

Hak mir nisht kain tsheinik.
Do not knock on my teakettle; in other words, stop pestering me.

Dinner will be ready when it's ready. *Hak mir nisht kain tsheinik.*

Halevei
If only! It should only be!

Maybe these new talks between the Israelis and Palestinians will succeed, *halevei*.

Khas v'khalilah
God forbid

Their son is in danger of flunking out of school, *khas v'khalilah*.

Khas vesholem
Heaven forbid

He is going to the doctor today for a stress test. I hope there's nothing wrong with his heart, *khas vesholem*.

Nechtiker tog

Literally, a night-like day; figuratively, yesterday's news

Stop *hak'n mir nisht kain tsheinik* about losing your keys. Forget about it already! *Nechtiker tog.* It is done and over with.

Pahst nisht

Inappropriate

They didn't invite their daughter's *makhatonim* to their anniversary party. *Pahst nisht.* It's just not the right way to act.

Shtinkt; Es shtinkt

Stinks

The school board just cut the music program. *Es shtinkt.*

Shande

Shame, scandal, embarrassment, [a public embarrassment, usually before the goyim (non-Jews) or the kinder (children); most commonly heard as in the following two examples:

Es iz a shande far di goyim.

It's an embarrassment in front of the non-Jews that he was arrested at the synagogue.

Es iz a shande far di kinder.

She just found out he has been shtupping his secretary and filed for divorce. It's a shame for the children.

A fremder nar iz a gleckhter; an aigener - a shand. - A strange fool is a laughing stock; your own - an embarrassment.

185

Shande un a kharpe A shame and a disgrace
The conditions in that nursing home are a shande un a kharpe.

Shandhoyz - Literally, house of shame, a whorehouse
I don't want my daughter to pledge that sorority. I heard it's nothing more than a *shandhoyz*.

Shund; Shund-roman
Trash; trashy novel
I have to admit that reading a *shand-roman* is one of my guilty pleasures.

VI. Superstitions

Jews, both Ashkenazim and Sephardim, have a lot of superstitions. Modern followers of Kabalah did not invent the red thread, nor were trendy urban architects the first to paint front doors blue. Both were designed in the Middle Ages as protective amulets to ward off the evil eye. Not all superstitions are negative, though.

Bashert
Predestined, intended; can be used for an event or a person.
As soon as they met, he knew she was his *bashert*. He asked her to marry him on their third date, and they've just celebrated their 55th anniversary.

It was *bashert* that I called my friend when I did - he just started a new business and offered me a job.

Az es bashert ainem dertrunken tzu verren vert her dertrunken in a leffel vasser. - If one is destined to drown, he will drown in a spoon of water.

Dybbuk

The soul or ghost of a deceased person who cannot find rest and inhabits the body of a living person.

That poor little girl in *The Exorcist* was possessed by a *dybbuk*.

In 1914, the writer S. Ansky penned a play in Russian, later translated into Yiddish, called *Der Dybbuk, oder Tzvishn Tzvei Veltn* (The Dybbuk, or Between Two Worlds). His story of a young bride possessed by the spirit of a suitor who had died of a broken heart when refused her hand in marriage was one of the most popular plays of the Yiddish theater. It premiered in Warsaw, as a tribute to Ansky, after his death in 1920. The next year, it was produced in New York by Maurice Schwartz of the Yiddish Art Theater. Shortly thereafter, it was translated into Hebrew by Hayim Nachman Bialik, Israel's leading poet, and performed in Moscow by Habima the National Theater of Israel, which continues to present *The Dybbuk*. The play was also made into a Yiddish-language film in Poland in 1937, and a ballet by Leonard Bernstein.

Gilgul

Reincarnation of a dead being, from the word for wheel.

She says her dog is the *gilgul* of her dead husband - he sleeps in the same bed with her, snores, steals the sheets, and pretends she's not there.

Golem

A creature formed from clay to protect the Jewish community of Prague; by analogy can refer to a person who's a dummy, doesn't think for himself.

Mary Shelley was familiar with the story of the *golem* when she wrote Frankenstein.

In England, they'd describe that *golem* as "thick as two planks."

Although there are many earlier references to the *Golem*, the first printed version of the famous story involving Rabbi Judah Loew of Prague appeared in *Galleri der Sippurim* (A Gallery of Stories) in 1847. Yudl Rosenberg's fictional account was published in 1909.

According to the story, the emperor threatened the Jewish community of Prague with expulsion or death. Rabbi Loew formed a human figure from clay, placed the word *emet* (truth) on its forehead, and by reciting incantations, breathed life into it. At first, the *Golem* protected the community, but then became more and more violent. The emperor begged Rabbi Loew, who was becoming concerned the *Golem* would turn on its creator, to destroy it. In return, the Jewish community would be allowed to live in peace. Rabbi Loew destroyed the *Golem* by erasing the first letter of *emet*, transforming the word into *met*, death. According to legend, the lifeless *Golem* is hidden in the *geniza*, the attic, of the Alte-Neue Shul (Old-New Synagogue) in Prague. The *geniza*, which is a traditional storehouse for damaged religious texts that cannot be used or destroyed (because they contain the name of God), is not open to the public.

Kenahora

The elision of the Hebrew phrase *k'neged ei'in harah*, against the evil eye; usually preceded or followed by spitting three times over one's shoulder or through one's open fingers. Since spitting is frowned upon in polite society, and is illegal in many public places, the phrase "tu-tu-tu" is substituted.

The baby is beautiful, *kenahora*. Tu-tu-tu.

Shaidim
Demons

Di gantzeh velt iz ful mit shaidim; treib zia khotsh fon zikh aroys.

The whole world is full of demons; you just exorcise them out of yourself.

Chapter Eleven

Shlemiels, Shlimazel, and Shlubs
How to Insult Someone

From the number of insults in Yiddish, you could get the impression that Eastern European Jews didn't like their neighbors very much. Or the elderly. Or bratty kids. Or fools. Or the lazy. Or gossips. Or those lacking social graces. Or snobs. Or hypocrites. Or even family members (their own or their neighbors').

In the comic strip *Pearls before Swine*, the character Rat is studying Yiddish because "I have determined it is by far the best language in the world for hurling insults." During the several days on which this theme ran in newspaper funny pages, Rat would utter nonsensical insults ("Stop being such a shmulky shlumperdik."), grammatically and linguistically accurate phrases ("Oy vey. Sorry to kvetch but this mishuganah's chutzpah has me pretty farklempt."), and combinations of both ("Tough talk from a Shabbes [sic] klopper schmendrick nudnik.")

One characteristic of Jewish humor is that it is self-deprecating. We laugh at ourselves to deflect the cruelty of others' scorn and to undercut the sting of their negative stereotypes. In the same way, when we insult others, we feel better about ourselves. And when people live in circumstances where they are considered subhuman, they need to use whatever tools they have to feel better about themselves. We insult others to undermine their ability to insult us.

Just as with curses, some of the most cutting insults are those that could be compliments. Who would be insulted to be called a *melamed*, a teacher of young children? Someone with aspirations to be a college professor would be - after all, if he's such a scholar, why is he teaching children?

And other words are considered insulting by the recipient, even though the speaker may not intend them to be. Goy, *shiksa*, *shaigitz*, shvartze all fall within this category. Another word is *faigele*, which literally means a little bird and is used to refer to a gay man. An older generation may have been heard to say, "Such a good-looking boy, but he is 40 years old already and never been married. Do you think he is maybe a [whispered] *faigele*?" (Of course, these same women would be the ones who would condemn idle gossip.)

So when you want to insult people without their knowing it, try some of these Yiddish words.

Alta makhsheife
Old witch
The *alte makhsheife* down the street gets angry whenever a young kid rides a Big Wheels trike in front of her house.

Alter tairekh
Old fool

Imagine taking karate at his age -- I wish he'd stop acting like an *alter tairekh*.

Alter trombenik
Old blowhard

That *alter trombenik* is always bragging about the great real estate deals he's made. So how come he's still living in the row house his parents bought in 1950?

Amoretz
From the Hebrew *am ha'aretz*, literally, person of the land; boor, ignoramus

He means well, but he's such an *amoretz*. I'm surprised he can function in real life.

Arumshlepper
A rootless person

I wish my grandson would find a good job already and stop being such an *arumshlepper*.

Azes punim
Such a face; said sarcastically about someone who is impudent, a wise guy.

There's a student in my class who shows no respect at all for authority. *Azes punim*.

Balagole
Literally, a wagon driver; boorish, vulgar type.

She's a lawyer. I don't understand what she sees in that *balagole*. I wouldn't be surprised if she's afraid of him.

Batlan
Idler
I don't know how my nephew's managing to stay in college. That *batlan* would rather play video games than study.

Ben kalba
Son of a bitch
I was waiting in line at the movie theater when a *ben kalba* cut into line and got the last ticket!

Dumkop
A dummy, a dolt, someone stupid
What kind of dumkop would try to light a barbecue grill using kerosene?

Farbissene
Crabby
I am sorry to be in a *farbissene* mood today, but I did not sleep well last night.

Farshimlt
Moldy
I hate going swimming with him. I don't think he ever washes his towels - they smell *farshimlt*.

Farshlepte krenk
Literally, a long illness; figuratively, an obnoxious person
Have you ever met such a *farshlepte krenk*? I hate having to work with her on this project. She

always acts as though everyone else is beneath her.

Farshlofener
Sluggard
Stop being a *farshlofener* and take out the trash already. How many times do I have to ask?

Farshluggine
Beaten up, ratty
This *farshluggine* car is always breaking down.
Mad Magazine's parody of the movie *Batman Forever* was called "Batman Farshlugginer."

Farshtunkene
Stinky
You broke your promise to help me out first thing this morning. A broken alarm clock is a *farshtunkene* excuse
A Scottish-born mystery author complained on Facebook that she had lost her wallet and then dropped her phone, while on a deadline for her new book. She wrote: "Getting a new smartphone up and running is definitely worse than replacing a wallet full of cards. But I'm still going to get this *farshluftige* book in." After some discussion, we decided she meant "farshtunkene book."

Farshvist
Sweaty

I hate hot flashes. I feel *farshvist* all the time.

Gridzhen
Literally, gnaw or chew noisily; figuratively, nag.
Stop *gridzhen* - I said I'll take out the trash, and I will. Later.

Hakhem
A wise man, a sage, used sarcastically to refer to a know-it-all
He thinks he such a *hakhem*, but he barely graduated from high school.

Khamoyer du ainer!
You ass!
Khamoyer du ainer! Look what you did to my car! Watch where you're going!

Khevraman
Happy-go-lucky, irresponsible
Sure, he's fun to be around, but I wouldn't count on that *khevraman* to complete any important task.

Khnyok
Bigot
Her father is such a *khnyok* that he refuses to accept his African-American son-in-law, even though he's Jewish.

Klafte
Bitch

That *klafte* at work told my supervisor that I had gone to lunch with my boyfriend instead of with a client.

Klainer gornisht
A little nothing

He thinks he's so important, but he's just a *klainer gornisht*.

K'negedacker
Big shot, know-it-all, braggart

I can't stand talking to that *k'negedacker*. He's always bragging.

Kokhleffel
Cooking ladle; figuratively one who "stirs the pot" with rumors or gossip.

If you want to know the dirt on anyone in the shul, just ask that *kokhleffel*. Her information might not be accurate, but it is juicy.

Kom vos er krikht.
Literally, come whatever, he crawls; figuratively, a slowpoke.

It makes sense for me to carpool with my neighbor, but he always makes me late for work. *Kom vos er krikht*. He'd be late for his own funeral.

Kundis
Brat

197

She thinks her son's a little angel, but he's a *kundis*

Laidikgaier
Literally, an empty walker; figuratively, an idler.

No one wants to do a team project with him because he's too much of a *laidikgaier*.

Lekish
Dummy, fool

Only a *lekish* would try to pay with an expired credit card.

Lemishke
Ineffectual

He's too much of a *lemishke* to be a good schoolteacher. The kids walk all over him.

Mamzer
Both literally and figuratively a bastard. In the legal sense, it refers to a child conceived through an adulterous relationship. In the colloquial sense, it is used the same as in English.

Can you believe that *mamzer* broke up with her just before her finals?

Az di muter shreit oyfen kind, "Mamzer!" meg men ir gloyben.

When a mother yells at her child, "Bastard!" you can believe her.

Mazik
Impish child

Her son is such a *mazik*, but he's so cute it's hard to stay angry at him.

Mieskeit
One who is ugly, homely
There's a lid for every pot and even a *mieskeit* like her can get married.

Melamed
A teacher of young children
He must not be too ambitious or smart if he's teaching kids.

The teaching profession is a noble one, and education is an important Jewish value, but there was an assumption in the Jewish world of Eastern Europe that if someone were truly learned he would have been teaching rabbinical scholars in a yeshiva, not young children in a *heder* (a one-room school). They were often poorly paid and itinerant. The same attitude exists in the United States, where elementary school teachers, particularly males, are not as highly regarded as high school teachers or, even better, college professors.

Meshugana; Meshuga, Meshugas
Crazy, nuts.
I can't wait until the elections are over. All these campaign ads are driving me meshugana.
Meshuga zol er vern un arumloyfn iber di gasn.
He should go nuts and run around through the streets.

Ven dos volt nit geven mein meshuganer, volt ikh oykh gelakht!

If he were not my madman, (if he were not related to me), I'd laugh at him, too.

Meshuga ahf toyt

Literally, crazy to death; figuratively, really nuts

I can't wait for the winter break to be over. Those kids are making me *meshuga ahf toyt*.

Anything that drives you meshugana is meshugas, which has a connotation of nonsense.

What do you mean you want to take a year off from college to be a roadie for a rock band? Stop talking such meshugas."

Nar; narishkeit

Fool; foolishness

Only a *nar* would give up a good paying job to go off to meditate at a commune in the middle of nowhere.

Leah Garrett interviewed *Mad* Magazine icon Al Jaffee for an article in the *Forward* called "How Mad Magazine Made American Humor Jewish."

"'So what is it you want to know?'" Jaffee asked me as I stood next to his big draftsman's table.

"I explained that I was working on a book about *Mad* and Jewish culture, so my first question was the obvious one: Why was there so much Yiddish in *Mad*?

"'Well, first of all, because I tend to think in Yiddish, and Yiddish conveys humor better than English.'

"'You still think in Yiddish then?' I asked.

"'It's *narishkeit*, but I still do,' he said with a chuckle."

Stop this *narishkeit* now! You are not getting a tattoo, and that's the end of it!

Tattoos and body piercings are frowned upon in Judaism, tattoos because they are considered to be a form of self-mutilation and an imitation of idolaters, and piercings because they are faddish and may interfere with personal hygiene.

In Leviticus 19:28, the Israelites were expressly forbidden from "writing a skin-etching" on themselves. In addition, since the Holocaust, when Jews in internment, slave labor, and extermination camps had registration numbers tattooed onto their arms, there is something almost obscene about voluntarily doing so.

Pierced ears are permitted for women because they are considered ornamentation. Many girls in Eastern Europe, Jews as well as non-Jews, had their ears pierced when they were infants.

Nishtikeit

A nothing

He thinks he's a big shot, but he's just a *nishtikeit*.

Nokhshlepper

Literally, one who drags along after; figuratively, a hanger-on

My little brother is always tagging along with my friends and me. I wish he'd get his own friends and stop being a *nokhshlepper*.

Noodge

Similar to a nudnik, a *noodge* is a persistent pain in the neck. Sometimes seen spelled as nudge, but that spelling is too similar for the English word that means to elbow someone or something out of the way. Most *noodges* can push you over the edge, though.

My son is being such a *noodge* about going to Disney World.

Ongebloozen

Sulking

She's fifteen, so of course she's always *ongebloozen*.

Ongeshtopf

Literally, overstuffed; figuratively, loaded with money

They're complaining they have to get a new car, but they can afford one. They are *ongeshtopf*.

Opgelozen

Careless dresser

I'm such an *opgelozen* - I went out today wearing two different colored shoes.

Oysgemutshet
Tired out
She's doing too much. She looks really *oysgemutshet*.

Oysshteler
Show off, braggart
The *oysshteler* in the next office spent the whole day talking about his new boat.

Oyverobotl
Absent minded
The say that forgetting where you put your keys is just being normally *oyverobotl*. Forgetting what a key is used for is more troubling.

Paskudne ; paskudnik; paskudnitze
Gross, nasty; a disgusting person
How can anyone be friends with that *paskudne*? Belushi was funny when he started the food fight in *Animal House*, but it's not funny in real life.

Paskudnik
Scoundrel
She found out the guy she was dating was engaged to someone else. What a *paskudnik*.

Pisher
Pishn means "to urinate," so a pisher is often used as an affectionate term of derision for a barely toilet trained toddler and, by extension, for

anyone who tries to do something beyond his ability.

That little *pisher* has been on the job for a week and already thinks he knows more than I do.

Potchke
Do too much, be obsessive

The house looks fine. Don't *potchke* so much.

Prust
Rough, coarse; socially unrefined

She may have grown up in a bad neighborhood, but she's not *prust*. She has really made something of herself.

Prustak
A vulgar person

He's a real *prustak*. He sees nothing wrong with swearing loudly in public.

Shikker
Drunkard

It's okay to have a drink once and a while, but he's a *shikker*. I don't think I've ever seen him sober.

Shlekht veib
Literally, a bad wife; figuratively, a shrew.

She better learn not to be a *shlekht veib* or her husband will look elsewhere for some appreciation.

Shmendrick

Fool, nincompoop, a pipsqueak

The early Woody Allen characters always acted like *shmendricks*.

Shtik holtz

Piece of wood; a person with no personality

Whenever a blind date isn't too attractive, she's described as having a nice personality. Well, this one is both a *mieskeit* and a *shtik holtz*.

Shtipper

Brat

I hate to say it about my sister, but her son is becoming a real *shtipper*. If he doesn't get what he wants, he has a temper tantrum until she gives in.

Shtunk

A stinker, a nasty person

His father's a real mensch, but he's a *shtunk*. After his father retires, I'm finding a different insurance agent.

Shvuntz

A coward

Don't be such a *shvuntz*. That dog's not going to bite you.

My grandmother, who was born in Ukraine, was frightened of dogs. It was almost a phobia. But there was a reality behind her fear that made it completely rational. Anti-Semites, including officially sanctioned police and soldiers, used vicious attack dogs to terrorize Jews.

Trombenik
A phony, a braggart

The *trombenik* down the street said he bought his wife a diamond tennis bracelet, but I saw him at the cubic zirconia counter at Wal-Mart the other day.

Tzatzke
Bauble (like *tchotchka*); figuratively, a cheap woman

Those skimpy clothes make her look like a *tzatzke*.

Umgelumpert
Awkward, clumsy

I feel sorry for my sixth grade students. The girls are becoming young women and the boys are still in the *umgelumpert* stage.

Vilde khei'a
Wild animal, a hyper child

Their son's a *vilde khei'*a, but their attitude is that boys will be boys.

Vilder mensch
A wild person

He never settled down, but is a *vilder mensch*, drinking, gambling, getting into fights.

Vontz

Literally, a bedbug; figuratively, a mischievous child

That *vontz* put salt into the sugar bowl.

One of the classic episodes of the television series *MASH* had a subplot featuring a crossword puzzle none of them could complete. The clue that had them stumped: Yiddish for "bedbug." The word was *vontz*.

Yakhne

A coarse, loud-mouthed woman; a gossip; a busybody

I bumped into that *yakhne* at the supermarket and I was so embarrassed by her braying laugh and insistence on telling me all about our neighbor's divorce.

Yetebedam

An intimidating man

I usually speak my mind, but that *yetebedam* scares me.

Yold

A yokel

I had to be nice to him because he's a customer, but when we went to lunch, the *yold* wiped his mouth on his sleeve.

Yungatch

A brat

He is a *yungatch* now, but a little discipline could set him straight.

Yutz

A stupid person

Don't be such a *yutz*. You understand exactly what I am saying.

Chapter Twelve

Lokn In Kop
The Basics of Body Language

There are, of course, Yiddish words for all the parts of the human body, as well as ones that are specific to male and female anatomy. Not surprisingly, many of the male and female body part words are considered obscene or, at the very least, vulgar, including seemingly benign euphemisms. Those words that are not acceptable in mixed (or not) company are listed in the next chapter on the "Dirtiest Yiddish" words. The ones below may be coarse, but can be said, if not in mixed company, then during casual conversations with those of the same gender.

Others words for the human body are also used to refer to chicken parts and other foods: pulkes, fis, gorgl, even tuchus (for the tail stump) are commonly heard. And some people love cow's tzung. The word kishke is interesting, as it changes meaning from a food item made with animal intestines to the actual intestines depending on whether the word is singular or plural.

Many of these body parts are the targets for Yiddish curses. How better to place a hex on enemies than by wishing them physical distress or harm? In the time before antibiotics and immunizations, any physical affliction could become fatal. A stomach cramp might be the result of too many onions fried in shmaltz, or could be a perforated ulcer or appendicitis. A broken bone could lead to permanent disability. Without teeth, one would not be able to enjoy most foods. Those who cast curses having to do with the body knew just how serious their threats were.

I. Human Anatomy

Bainer
Bones
A kholaire im zain bainer.
A cholera in his bones.
Shtainer ahf zeine bainer.
Stones on his bones.
Zol di markh oprinen fon deine bainer.
Your bones should be drained of marrow.
Zolst tze brekhn alle deine bainer az oft mol vi di brekhtz di aseres hadibres.
You should break your bones as often as you break the Ten Commandments.

Boykh
Belly, stomach
A kapn im in zain boykh.
A cramp in his stomach!
A makeh im zein boykh, a ruekh in zein tatns tate arein.
A plague in his belly, a devil in his father's father.
Az der boykh iz laidik iz her moy'akh oylk laidik.
When the stomach is empty, so is the brain.

Es zol dir dunern in boykh, vestu maien az s'iz a homon klaper.

Your stomach will rumble so badly, you'll think it was Purim noisemaker.

Zi iz geven a kurveh in di mames boykh.

She was a whore in her mother's stomach.

Zol dikh kapn beim boykh.

You should get a stomach cramp.

Fis

Foot

Some cooks like to throw the chicken *fis* into the soup pot, but at least they remove them before serving the soup.

Zol er tzebrekhen a fis.

He should break a leg.

Gederem

Bowels

A kapn in di gederem!

A cramp in his bowels!

Gorgl

Neck, throat

She's had a face lift and uses Botox, but her scrawny *gorgl* gives away her age.

I think I am coming down with something. My *gorgl* hurts. Maybe I should gargle?

Helzel

A dish similar to *kishke*, but the casing is made from the chicken's neck rather than the intestines.

My aunt made *helzel*, but I don't think she ever made *kishke*.

Kishke
Stuffed derma.

In addition to the dish called stuffed derma in English, kishkes means intestines. Even though stuffed derma sounds more appealing than stuffed intestines, the words are synonyms. In fact, the etymology of derma is the Yiddish word derme, the plural of darm, another word for intestine.

Zol er hobn a kapn im di kishkes.

He should have a cramp in his guts.

Kop
Head

Alle tzoris vos ikh hob oyf mein hartzn, zoln oysgain tzu zein kop.

All problems I have in my heart, should go to his head.

Drai mir nit kain kop.

Literally, do not twist my head; figuratively, stop pestering me.

Fardrai zikh dem kop.

Literally, turn your head; figuratively, drive yourself crazy.

Gai shlog dein kop in vant.

Go bang your head on the wall.

Klap en kop.

Hit on the head, as in "If you don't behave, I'll give you a *klap en kop*."

Lokh in kop.

A hole in the head, as in the oft-heard Yiddishism "I need it like a *lokh in kop.*"

Zol dir klapn in kop.

It should bang in your head; may it only happen to you like to me.

Zol er lebn bis hundert un tzvantzik yor - on a kop.

He should live to 120 years - without a head.

Lipelakh

Lips

He has *dininke lipelakh*, and you can't trust anyone with thin lips.

Moyl

Mouth

A kleine veibeleh ken oykh hoben a groysse moyl.

A small wife can also have a big mouth.

Farmakh dos moyl.

Shut your mouth.

Nem on a fuln moyl vaser!

Literally, fill up your mouth with water; figuratively, keep your mouth shut.

Oygn

Eyes

Baide oygn deine zoln faln fon dein kop, khas vesholem.

Both your eyes should fall out of your head, God forbid.

Zaltz im in di oygn, feffer im in di noz.

Throw salt in his eyes, pepper in his nose.

Pulkes

Legs, thighs, usually plump ones

Fat *pulkes* are cute on a baby, but not on a grown woman wearing a bikini.

Don't eat the chicken *pulkes*. I'm saving them for the kids. If they don't want them, I'll cut them (the pulkes, not the kids!) up and throw them into the chicken zup.

Tzainer

Teeth. There are two versions of the same curse:

Zolst farlirn alle tzainer akhutz ainem, un der zol dir vai ton.

You should lose all your teeth except one, and that one should ache!

Zolst farlirn alle deine tzainer akhutz ainer, un in dem zolst hobn a shreklikher tzainvaitik.

You should lose all your teeth but one, and you should have a terrible toothache in it.

Tzung

Tongue

I never liked *tzung*. It looks too much like a cow's tongue, which is what it is.

A behaimeh hot a langen tzung un ken nicht redden; der mensch hot a kurtzeh tzung un tor nisht reden.

An animal has a long tongue and can't speak; a man has a short tongue and shouldn't speak.

A hiltzener tzung zol er bakumn.

He should grow a wooden tongue.

Du host a langer tzung!

Literally, you have a long tongue; figuratively, you have a big mouth.

Got zol gebn, er zol hobn altzding vos zein hartz glist, nor er zol zein gelaimt oyf alle eivers un nit kenen rirn mit der tzung.

God should bestow him with everything his heart desires, but he should be a quadriplegic and not be able to use his tongue.

Hinten

Rear end, buttocks, ass; the word is synonymous with tuchus, but tuchus is used only to refer to the buttocks, while *hinten* can also be used as a direction, just as "rear" in English can refer to either the body part or the direction.

Move to the *hinten*.

Vifil yor er iz gegangn oyf di fis zol er gain ahf di hent un di iberike zol er zikh sharn oyf di hinten.

As many years as he has walked on his feet, he should walk on his hands, and for the rest of the time he should crawl along on his ass.

Pupik

Bellybutton, naval. Often pronounced "pipik."

Can you believe all these young girls walking around with their *pupiks* hanging out?

Zol vaks tzibeles fon dein pupik.

Onions should grow from your bellybutton.

Shnoz

A nose, usually a long one. Sometimes called a shnozzola.

Jimmy Durante, or if you prefer your cultural references to be literary, Cyrano de Bergerac, had the epitome of the shnoz.

I came across two interesting variations of shnoz:

In front of Grauman's Chinese Theater, Jimmy Durante's nose print is preserved in cement with the notation, "Dis is my schnozzle."

In his 2007 novel, *The Yiddish Policeman's Union*, Michael Chabon used noz, a variation of, shnoz, as slang for a police detective.

Tuchus

Rear end, buttocks. Anglicized as tush.

Stop being such a pain in the tuchus.

I worked my tuchus off for that company and then they treated me like a *khei kak*.

A tuchus un a halb. - Literally, a rear end and a half; figuratively, a voluptuous woman.

I don't like skinny women. I prefer one with a *tuchus un a halb*.

A friend told me that her grandmother had a saying for everything. One of her favorites was "Never let your husband see more than half a tuchus." In other words, keep some mystery in your marriage. Or, to be more cynical, you don't have to tell him everything.

Kush mir in tuchus! - Kiss my ass!

Mel Blanc, who provided the voices for almost all the Loony Toons characters, had a license plate with the letters KMIT. When the official from the California Department of Motor Vehicles questioned him as to its meaning, Blanc said it stood for an old Jewish expression, "Know Me in Truth." It actually stood for *Kush Mir in tuchus*.

Shtup es in tuchus. - Shove it up your ass.

Tuchus ahfen tish! - Ass on the table! Put up or shut up! (In English, we'd say, "Shit or get off the pot.")

Zolst lebn vi a tzibele, mit dein kop in drerd und dein tuchus in di luft.

You should live like an onion, with your head in the ground and your ass in the air.

Zaftig

Pleasingly plump.

A *Yiddishe maidl* (Jewish maiden) should be zaftig and have some meat on her bones, not like those scarecrows you see on TV.

II. Male Anatomy

Of course, there are words that are only for men.

Baitzim

Testicles, from the Hebrew for "eggs;" a synonym for chutzpah, in the same way that "balls" and "nerve" can be used interchangeably in English.

I could not believe the *baitzim* on that guy, talking back to the traffic cop like that.

Petzeleh

Little penis, usually derogatory, but can be used affectionately to refer to a toddler. From the Yiddish word *pitzel* (wee, tiny).

Look at that *petzeleh* trying to imitate his older brother. He is so cute.

Shvantz
Penis
I have never seen an uncircumcised *shvantz*.

III. Female Anatomy

And there are words used only for women.

Bristen
Breasts
It's a fallacy that all Jewish women have large *bristen*.

Just as there are a lot of euphemisms and synonyms for "penis," so are there many for "vagina." All the following are ways to refer to a woman's private parts.

Dorten
Down there
She had to have surgery *dorten* for female problems.

K'negedipl

Literally, the corner of a handerkerchief; figuratively, a nest egg; euphemistically, a hymen.

Her new husband was inexperienced, so she was able to fool him into thinking she still had an intact *k'negedipl*.

Oysoy hamokom

Literally, that place, a woman's privates.

I have got an itch *oysoy hamoko*m. It must be a yeast infection.

Chapter Thirteen

Triken A Fortz
The Dirtiest Yiddish

The words below are considered obscene, vulgar, and coarse. Other words in the book are too, but these are the ones most likely to get your mouth washed out with soap. It is doubtful your Bubbe - or even your Zaide - ever used them, and they may not have even known them. At the very least, they'd never have admitted to knowing them.

Several of these words, among them drek, putz, and shlong, are used by English speakers who have an idea of what they mean but don't realize they are considered obscene in Yiddish. There's a certain irony that English speakers use these words to avoid using what they consider the more taboo Anglo-Saxon ones.

Some of these words have to do with defecation, some with the euphemisms used for male and female genitalia, and the rest, of course, with sex and sexual intercourse.

The Yiddish word for sex is *geshlekht*. It is not etymologically related to *shlekht*, which means bad. In fact, in Judaism, sex is seen as a positive act, and it is even a double mitzvah for a married couple to have sex on Shabbos. One of the promises a groom makes to his bride - a promise codified in the *kesubah* (marriage contract) - is sexual gratification. It is even said that if a man wants to conceive a son, he should

221

make sure his wife has an orgasm. (And it may not be just superstition: there is modern scientific evidence that the contractions of a woman's vaginal muscles during orgasm help move the sperm along to their targeted egg.)

So next time you want to be "naughty," but not use the English equivalents, try one of these words:

I. Defecation

Drek
Shit; human dung, feces, manure or excrement; inferior merchandise or work; insincere talk or excessive flattery
Drek ahf dem teller.
Literally, shit on a plate; figuratively, worthless.
Drek mit leber.
Literally, shit with liver; figuratively, worthless.
Shtik drek.
Piece of shit; shit-head.

Fortz
Literally, fart; figuratively a jerk
He is such a *fortz*. There is nothing about him I like.
Du zolst nor fortzn in drerd.
You should only fart in the ground (in other words, in your grave).
Oder a klop oder a fortz.

Literally, either a wallop or a fart. In other words, either too much or not enough, similar to "feast or famine" in English.

Trikhen a fortz. - Dried old fart

Kak

Crap

Alter Kaker

Old fart, often abbreviated by English speakers as A.K.

When we went back to the college for our 40th reunion, we realized we are now officially A.K.'s.

Kak im on

Defecate on him! (The hell with him!)

Farkakt

Shitty, crappy, fucked up; from kak.

If this *farkakte* photocopier doesn't stop jamming, I'll never get the reports done in time for the board meeting.

Kak zikh oys!

Go shit on yourself

Khei kak. Nothing, infinitesimal, worthless, unimportant; literally human dung

II. Body Parts

Shmuck

An asshole, a fool; derisive term for a man; from an obscene slang word for penis.

That shmuck saw me waiting for that parking spot, but snuck in around me.

Tuchusleker

Literally, ass licker; figuratively, a brown-noser, apple-polisher, ass-kisser.

You don't think he got the promotion on merit, do you? He's nothing but a *tuchusleker*.

III. Male Genitalia

Putz

Slang for penis, derogatory term for someone who's not very nice.

He took credit for his associate's work. What a putz.

Aus der putz shteyt, der seychel gait.

When the prick stands up, reason departs.

Er muz zein a yamputz, veil ahf der yaboshe hob ikh nit gezen aza ainem.

He must be a sea prick, because I have never seen such a prick on dry land.

Groysser putz

Big penis; big prick. Always said in a derogatory or sarcastic manner, never as a description of physical attributes.

My supervisor is a *groysser putz* - he refused to let his secretary leave early when her son was sent home sick from school.

Putznasher

Cocksucker

Get out of my way! *Putznasher*!

Shlong

Literally, a snake, serpent; figuratively, a penis.

Did you see the *shlong* on that horse! I wonder if the owner gets large stud fees.

IV Female Genitalia

K'nish

An Eastern European pastry dish, dough filled with meat, potatoes, cheese, or other foods. Also a euphemism for female genitalia.

Heh, I know what I'd like to stuff her k'nish with.

After my teenaged son found out the other meaning of k'nish, he couldn't hear the word without sniggering.

Pirge

A meat pie or dumpling, similar to the Polish piroge (or to a k'nish); used like "pussy" in English.

Hey, *tzatzke*, let me see your *pirge*.

Zakh; spiel zakh.

Literally, thing, plaything; figuratively, an obscene euphemism for female privates.

Let's go out tonight and see if we can score a *spiel zakh*.

V. Sex

Baren

Fornicate, fuck with; figuratively, to bother, annoy.

Baren with Don Corleone, and you'll find a horse's head in your bed.

Dusik
Slightly fucked up
I have to go see my boss. The vacation schedule came out and is *dusik*

Eingefedemt
Literally, to thread a needle; a euphemism for sexual intercourse.
Er hot kainmol nit eingefedemt. - He has never been with a woman.

Hais, kalt
Hot, cold
Ikh bin hais. - I am hot, I am horny.
Ikh bin kalt.
I am cold, I am frigid.
As in many languages, including Hebrew and German, to say the temperature is making you shiver or sweat, you use the equivalent of "It is hot to me," and "It is cold to me." Otherwise, you're talking about your libido not the weather.

Makhen a mitzvah
To do a good deed; a euphemism for having sex (usually within marriage).
The kids are all at friends' houses tonight, so we use the time to *makhen a mitzvah*.

Meise

Literally, a story or tale, a deed; figuratively, an obscene euphemism for intercourse, similar to the English phrase, "I did her."

So, how was your date last night? Did you do the *meise*?

Shtup

Push, shove. One of many euphemisms for sexual intercourse.

Nu, do you think you'll get to *shtup* her tonight?

Trenen

Literally, to rip, rend, open a seam; figuratively, to screw, engage in the act of intercourse.

I had an awful cold and just wanted to *gai shlufen*, but my boyfriend wanted to *trenen*. I gave him a choice - leave me alone or sleep on the couch.

Gai tren zkh. - Go fuck yourself.

Yentzen

To fornicate, to whore, to screw in the metaphorical sense

My boss tried to *yentzen* me out of my bonus.

VI. Prostitution

There are two words for prostitutes, both of which are used as descriptions of professionals and as insults.

Kurveh

Whore, prostitute

My husband ran off with that *kurveh*. We'll see how long she stays with him after my lawyer finishes taking him for all he is worth.

Nafkeh

Prostitute

What kind of role model for young teenaged girls is that actress? She looks like a *nafkeh*.

It is not generally known that Jews were involved in the thriving international "white slave trade." Young, naïve Eastern European Jewish women would be promised jobs, and then forced to work in brothels. Others would fall for the charms of a handsome young man who would marry them, and then give them a ticket to Buenos Aires, saying he would meet them there later. In Argentina, they would be met by the madam, who, claiming to be the young man's aunt, would take them home with her and gradually introduce them to the realities of their new lives: sell your body or starve.

Shunned by the Argentinian Jewish community, these women could not be buried in the Jewish cemeteries, and established their own burial society, in 1916, called the Jewish Benevolent and Burial Association, popularly known as the Society of Truth. The last burial there was in 1970.

Sholem Aleichem wrote a short story in 1909 called *A Mentsh fon Buenos-Ayres* (The Man from Buenos Aires). It was about a Jewish "salesman" from Argentina named Motek, who said of the goods he sold: "I supply the world with merchandise, something that everybody knows and nobody speaks of ...What do I deal in? Not in prayer books, my friend, not in prayer books."

Of course, these illegal activities, and the existence of large Jewish crime syndicates, led to increased anti-Semitism and promoted the stereotypes of Jews as corrupters of morals and despoilers of young women. According to some sources, the Portuguese word for pimp, cafetão, comes from kaftan, the long black silk robe worn by some Orthodox Jews.

There are two other words for whorehouse besides *shandhoyz*.

Heizel
Whorehouse
There are so many different men going in and out of that apartment that I wonder if it is a *heizel*.

Nafkeh bais
Whorehouse
Did you see the news? They raided that message parlor down the street. It was a front for a *nafkeh bais*.

Jewish prostitutes accounted for seventeen percent of known prostitutes in Warsaw in 1872. In Krakow, the number was twenty-seven percent, and in Vilna forty-seven percent. By 1889 Jewish women ran seventy percent of the licensed brothels in the Jewish Pale.

Chapter Fourteen

Oy, Ikh Darf Zikh Oyspishn Geferlekh
Other Useful Words

There are quite a few other Yiddish words that can be interspersed in conversation to make it more interesting. Some will be familiar to English speakers, while others will cause your listeners to mentally shrug and think: 1. You are a brilliant and erudite multi-linguist; 2. You are a pretentious (is there any other kind?) poser; or 3. You have no idea what you're talking about. I would not recommend using too many of these expressions with someone who may be familiar with Yiddish, as that person might strike up an entire conversation with you in that language. If that should happen, look thoughtful, nod, occasionally shrug and say, "Nu," and try to escape before the Yiddish speaker realizes you haven't understood a word.

The words that follow are in common usage, and with the exception of the bodily functions, are everyday objects, events or places. Again, except for those words dealing with bodily functions, most of them are not vulgarisms, but part of daily life: clothing, school, synagogue, family relationships, religious rituals, expressions. Without knowing them, you will not understand the references many Jews make, whether in person or in the media.

In earlier generations, no one needed to be taught how to keep a kosher home; it was ingrained from youth and observed as a matter of course. Synagogue and home religious rituals were learned through example and practice, not by attendance at the occasional holiday service or by going to religious school a couple of hours a week, if it didn't conflict with soccer.

Of course, these are generalizations. There were plenty of Yiddish speakers who were not religious, did not wear "Jewish" clothing, ate pork, worked on Shabbos. There were differences between those who lived in a crowded city ghetto and those in a rural, remote shtetl, those who chose to remain in Europe and those who sought a new and, they hoped, safer and more prosperous life in the United States, those whose political biases led them to improve conditions in their countries of origin and those who established a new country on the remains of the ancient Jewish homeland.

But the one thing that bound them together was the Yiddish language.

I. Bodily Functions

Quite a few expressions have to do with evacuation of bodily fluids (a nice way of saying "crapping, pissing, and barfing").

Brekhn

To vomit. (Same word is used for "to break.")

Men ken brekhn. - It can make you vomit.

Cristiyah

Enema

I'd rather eat a box of prunes than have a *cristiyah*.

Dusn

Literally, this; euphemism for shit.

What a mess! Clean up the *dusn*.

Greps

Belch, burp, hiccups, heart burn.

I love peppers but they give me *greps*.

The best way to get rid of *greps* is a spoon of sugar.

Kaneh

An enema

He was so embarrassed before his surgery when they gave him a *kaneh*.

Pishekhtz

Urine

I wish my boyfriend would learn how to aim. The bathroom always smells like *pishekhtz*.

Pishn; oyspishn

To urinate

Ikh darf zikh oyspishn.

I have to take a leak.

Oy, ikh darf zikh oyspishn - geferlekh!
Boy, do I need to take a leak something fierce!

There are, of course, other functions that nothing to do with elimination.

Bankes
Blood
Toyten bankes
Toyten means "dead" and the word bankes also refers to suction cups used medically to bring the blood to the surface for blood letting.
Es vet helfen vi a toyten bankes.
It will help like taking blood from a corpse.

Deige
Worry, concern
Ein deige
Literally, one worry; figuratively, health
He goes to doctors all the time. He's obsessed with his *eyn deige.*
Melokheh bez deige.
To have a trade is to be free of worry.
Nit gedeiget
Not to worry
I panicked when my mother called me at midnight, but she said, "*Nit gedeiget* . Everything's fine."

Kvitsh
Shriek, screech
She gave a loud *kvitsh* when she saw a rat.

Shluf
Sleep
Gai shlufn. - Go to sleep.

Shmeikhl
Literally, smile; figuratively, smooth talk.

He has such a beautiful *shmeikhl* that it's easy to fall for his shtik.

His *shmeikhl* almost convinced me to go out with him.

Shokl
To rock back and forth rhythmically; used to describe movement during prayer.

Stand still and don't *shokl*. You're not in shul.

Shpilkes
Literally, nails; figuratively, to be impatient.

I can't take my husband to see a "chick flick." He gets *shpilkes*.

Sitzflaish
Literally, sitting flesh; figuratively, patience.

It is going to be a long wait. We'll need some *sitzflaish* or we'll get *shpilkes*.

II. Jewish Fashion

It should not be surprising that many of the words for common items of clothing have a religious basis, as religion was central to Jewish life in Eastern Europe. It was just a fact of life, not a matter of philosophical or theological discussion, for all but the Talmudic scholars and their students. A married woman did not consider the feminist implications of keeping her hair covered in the presence of men other than her husband. The kind of clothing a man wore could identify him at a glance as belong to a particular Chasidic sect.

Gatkes

This word describes an article of clothing that is not religious, but is necessary in a cold climate: long underwear.

It was a good thing I had put on my *gatkes* before going out today, or I'd have frozen my tuchus off.

Kapote

Long coat, kaftan (but not the kind that large size women wear when they want to be comfortable).

The *kapote* some ultra-Orthodox men wear is modeled on the clothing worn by Medieval Polish nobility.

Kittel

A plain white robe, made of cotton or linen, worn on the High Holy Days. A groom who is traditional will often wear a kittel for the ceremony.

He's so cheap, he wore a kittel when he got married, even though he's not Orthodox. That way he got out of hiring a tux!

Pai'is

Side curls worn by Chasidic men in obedience to the law in the Torah not to cut the corners of one's beard.

When he goes out in public, he tucks his *pai'is* behind his ears. It seems hypocritical to me.

Shaitl

A wig worn by Orthodox women after they marry.

I don't understand how a *shaitl* can be a sign of modesty when some of them are sexier looking than the woman's real hair!

Shmatte

A rag; used to refer to clothing. The word lent itself to a whole industry.

Put on a nice dress. You are not wearing that *shmatte* on the first day of school.

Many new immigrants went into the *shmatte* trade on the Lower East Side.

Tichel

A headscarf

Instead of cutting her hair short and wearing a *shaitl*, she covers her head with a *tichel* when she's in public. She thinks she looks like a hippie, but she just looks frumpy.

Yarmulke

A skullcap, worn by most Jews during worship and by Orthodox Jews all the time.

It's a yarmulke, not a beanie.

In Western culture, it is traditional for men to remove their hats indoors or in the presence of superiors, to show respect and/or humility. In Eastern cultures, however, a head covering is a symbol of reverence and/or subservience, often to God. When the two cultures collide, misunderstandings, discrimination, and persecution can result. In 1986, for example, the Supreme Court ruled in favor of the Air Force, which forbad a Jewish chaplain from wearing a yarmulke while in uniform.

In 2004 in a small Delaware town, a Jewish family was harassed after complaining that the pastor offering the invocation at their daughter's high school graduation, where she was the only Jewish student, said: "I also pray for one specific student, that You be with her and guide her in the path that You have for her. And we ask all these things in Jesus' name." Their son wore a yarmulke and, according newspaper accounts, during a public hearing on the complaint, the crowd heckled the sixth grader to take his yarmulke off. The account continued: "Classmates accused [him] of 'killing Christ' and he became fearful about wearing his yarmulke, the complaint recounts. He took it off whenever he saw a police officer, fearing that the officer might see it and pull over his mother's car. When the family went grocery shopping, the complaint says, '[He] would remove the pin holding his yarmulke on his head for fear that someone would grab it and rip out some of his hair.'"

It is not only Jews who have been forbidden from wearing head coverings, but also Sikhs and Moslems. After the attacks of September 11, 2001, the prejudice became even more pronounced.

III. Family Matters

And family does matter.

Ainikl
Grandchild
She hopes her *ainikl* will give her son as much trouble as he gave her.

Bubbe and Zaide
Grandmother and grandfather
When your parents say, "No," ask Bubbe. If she says, "No," ask Zaide. He is a real pushover.

Bubbe *meises*
Literally "grandmother stories," which refers to fairy tales or old wives' tales.
It's a bubbe *meise* that you'll catch a cold if you go outside without wearing a coat.

Bubele
A casual term of endearment, often used by people who are trying to establish an ersatz intimacy; sweetie pie
Listen, *bubele*, I wouldn't lie to you. You won't find a better deal anywhere.

Ganze mishpokha
The whole family
Instead of enjoying his surprise birthday party, he got angry because the *ganze mishpokha* wasn't invited.

Kaddishl
Little Kaddish
After having given birth to several daughters, his wife finally gave him a kadddishl.
Mein tei'erer kaddishl - My dear little Kaddish
Mein tei'erer kaddishl is about to become a father himself.
The Kaddish is known as the Mourner's Prayer, even though it is actually a paean of praise to God. It is recited by the deceased's closest relatives, mainly the spouse, the children, and siblings, although friends will often say it as well, especially during shiva, the seven days of mourning following the funeral. Traditionally, Kaddish was recited by males only, so kaddishl was a way of referring to sons.

Kindelakh
Little children.
I love having my cousins visit, but their *kindelakh* are out of control.

Mamaleh
Little mother, used as a term of endearment or exasperation

Look at her taking care of her doll. Such a sweet *mamaleh*.

Hey, *mamaleh*, move your cart out of the middle of the aisle.

Oy, *mamaleh*, I got such a headache, you would not believe!

Tante

Aunt, can be used for a blood relative or for a close friend of one's parents.

I've never been able to figure out who's an aunt, who's a cousin, and who's my mother's friend. Eveyone one is called tante.

Tateh
Father
My tateh was nothing like Ozzie Nelson!
Tateh-Mama
Literally, father-mother; refers to parents.

Barukh Hashem, my tateh-mama are still healthy.

She has a great relationship with her tateh-mama - they live on the other side of the country.

Yingele
Youngster
You're too old to shovel the snow yourself. Hire the *yingele* next door to do it for you.

Yiddishe Mama

Literally, a Jewish mother, but refers more to a specific type of woman: warm, nurturing, and a bit smothering.

241

Gertrude Berg in the early '50s TV show *The Goldbergs* was the first Yiddishe mama most of Middle America had ever invited into their living rooms.

One of the most beloved Yiddish songs of all time is *A Yiddish Mama*, written by composer Jack Yellin and lyricist Lou Pollack. It produces the same sentimental reaction in Jewish listeners as *Danny Boy* does in Irish ones.

Yortzeit

Literally, time of year; refers to the anniversary of a death

He forgot his father's *yortzeit* and his mother won't talk to him. To him, that's a *mekhei'ya*.

IV. Miscellaneous

Bentshn

To make a blessing, usually after meals or over candles, but can be used as well in curses.

After spending the summer at a Jewish camp, my son began to *bentsh* after meals. But he didn't know the words, so it sounded like gibberish.

Got zol im bentshn mit drei mentshn: ainer zol im haltn, der tzvaiter zol im shpaltn un der driter zol im ba'haltn.

God should bless him with three people: one should grab him, the second should stab him and the third should hide him.

Der zach
Literally, the thing; figuratively, whatchamacallit

Hand me the ... um ... you know what I mean, *der zach* over there.

Emes
Truth
A halber emes iz a gantzer ligen.
A half truth is a whole lie.
A ligen tor men nit zogen; dem emes iz men nit mekuyev zogen.
A lie shouldn't be told; the truth doesn't have to be told.
A ligner glaibt men nit, afileh az er zogt dem emes.
No one believes a liar even when he tells the truth.
Der emes hot a sakh punimer.
The truth has many faces.
Di ergsteh rekhiles iz der emes.
The worst libel is the truth.

Ganze Megillah
The whole story, in detail. The word megillah is Hebrew for scroll, and is most often used to refer to the Book of Esther (*Megillas* Esther).

I made the mistake of asking him what he did on his vacation, and I got stuck listening to him for an hour as he gave me the *ganze Megillah*.

Get

Divorce decree, issued by rabbinic authorities to dissolve a marriage.

A week after the wedding, and he already wanted to give her a *get*.

In traditional Judaism, only a man can issue a divorce decree to his wife. If he refused, his wife would never be able to remarry and if she did, her children would be *mamzerim* (bastards). He, however, would be allowed to remarry, as in Biblical times men were allowed to have more than one wife. A woman in this situation is called an agunah, or a "chained woman." She and her family are often subject to what amounts to extortion by the husband so he will release her. There are many modern attempts to rectify this injustice within the bounds of Jewish law (*halakhah*).

Glatt azoy

Plainly, just so, for no reason

Why do I want to take dance lessons? No particular reason, *glatt azoy*.

In mitn drinen

In the middle of

The professor was telling us what would be on the final when *mitn drinen* there was a fire drill.

Likht

Light; holiday or Shabbos candles

Every Friday night, my mother would *bentch likht*. Then we'd go out to dinner.

Luftmensch

Someone who walks with his head in the air, a dreamer (but not an airhead)

My philosophy professor is a real *luftmensch*. He'll stop talking in the middle of a lecture because he's thought of something else, and then he'll walk out of the classroom muttering to himself without remembering we're still in class.

Oht azoy

Thusly

I showed you a dozen times how to do it - *oht azoy*, just like that.

Shtiebl

A small synagogue

Every time he would have a fight with the rabbi, he'd join another *shtiebl* .

Takhlis

Purpose, aim, heart of the matter.

I hate these meetings that go on and on with everybody having to give a long-winded speech. I wish they'd get down to *tachlis* already.

Takeh

An untranslatable interjection similar to "really?" or "come on."

So, *takeh*, what happened on your blind date? I want the *ganze megillah*.

Vo den?

"What then?"

Vo den? Don't leave me in suspense. Finish the story.

Vos macht du?

Literally, What makes you? In other words, "How are you?"

I haven't seen you in ages. *Vos macht du*?

Yahupitz

Middle of nowhere, Hicksville.

I have no idea where they live, somewhere in *yahupitz*.

Acknowledgements
First Edition

My appreciation goes to Paula Munier, acquisitions editor of Adams Media, who had faith that I could write this book, and to her assistant, Sara Stock, who shepherded me through the process.

My thanks to those who did not want to be acknowledged by name, but gave me words and phrases and advice.

Thanks to my mother, whose own mother was more comfortable speaking in Yiddish than English, for her memories of her childhood. And to my father who, despite having grown up with parents who did not speak Yiddish and a grandmother who did not want to speak it, still picked up a lot of phrases.

And profound, deep gratitude to my husband, Rabbi Gary M. Gans, who proofread the manuscript, and gave me ideas and suggestions, and caught all my typos. I could not have produced this book without him.

Ilene Schneider ,2008

Second Edition

There are two additional thanks to be added. First, to Michael Orenduff, author of the Pot Thief mystery series, owner of Book and Table in Valdosta, GA, editor and publisher with Aakenbaaken and Kent, who accepted the challenge of proofreading, formatting, and publishing this revised editon. Second, to all those who bought the original book, both for themselves and as gifts, and read, enjoyed, reviewed, and shared with me their reactions and suggestions.

Ilene Schneider, 2017

Glossaries

I. Glossary of Words and Phrases

Literal translations are given first. Figurative meanings are in brackets.

Agunah - a woman whose husband refuses to give her a divorce [chained wife]

Ainikl - a grandchild

Alef-bais - alphabet

Alta makhsheife - old witch

Alta moyd - an old maid

Alter bokher - a bachelor

Alter kaker- an old fart [also called an A.K.]

Alter tairekh - old fool

Alter trombenik - old blowhard

Amoretz - a person of the land [boor, ignoramus]

Apikoros - a heretic

Arbeiter Ring - Workman's Circle

Aroysgevorfene gelt - wasted money [throwing good money after bad]

Arumgeflikt - plucked on all sides [robbed, swindled]

Arumshlepper - a rootless person

Ashkenaz - Northern, Central, and Eastern Europe

Ashkenazi - a Jew from Northern, Central, or Eastern Europe

Auf tzolokes - bad luck

Auf tzoris - in big trouble

Aufruf - synagogue service honoring a couple on Shabbos before the wedding

Az okh un vai - tough luck

Azes punim - such a face [one who is impudent, rude]

Babke - a pastry

Badkhan - an entertainer

Bagel - a small round bread product with hole in middle

Bainer - bones

Baitzim - testicles (from Hebrew for "eggs")

Balabost - a boss

Balagan - a noisy tumult [a mess]

Balagole - a vulgar type

Balboosta - a housewife

Bankes - blood

Bar Mitzvah - boy who has reached the age of maturity [ceremony to mark the event]

Baren [obscene] - fornicate; bother, annoy

Barukh Hashem - thank God

Bas Mitzvah - a girl who has reached the age of maturity [ceremony to mark the event]

Bashert - predestined

Batempt - tasty

Batlan - an idler

Behaima - a beast, ogre

Bekher - a goblet

Ben kalba - son of a bitch

Bentshn - to recite the Grace after Meals

Besulah - a never married woman

Bialy - a roll similar to a bagel but without a hole

Bilik - inexpensive

Bis hundert un tzvantzik yor - until a hundred and twenty years

Blintz - similar to a crepe, rolled and filled with cheese or fruit

Bokher - a boy, youngster

Borscht - beet soup

Borzhvaz - Bourgeois

Boykh - stomach, belly

Brekhn - to vomit [also "to break"]

Brenen - to burn

Bris milah (or Bris) - circumcision

Bristen - breasts

Brokh - a curse

Bronfn - whiskey

Bubbe - grandmother

Bubbe meiseh - an old wives' tale.

Bubele - sweetie pie

Bupkis - nothing

Challah - an egg bread, often braided, for Shabbos

Chanukah - Festival of Lights

Chasidim - traditional Jews who follow the teachings of specific rebbes

Chutzpah - nerve, guts

Cristiyah - an enema

Deige - worry, concern

Der zach - the thing [whatchamacallit]

Dorten - down there (euphemism for female privates)

Draidel - a spinning top

Draikop - one who turns heads [finagler]

Drek- shit, excrement [inferior merchandise or work; insincere talk or excessive flattery]

Drek ahf dem teller - shit on a plate [worthless]

Drek mit leber - shit with liver [worthless]

Dumkop - dumb head [a dummy, idiot]

Dusik - slightly fucked up

Dusn - this [euphemism for shit]

Dybbuk - a ghost

Ein deige - one worry [health]

Eingefedemt - tto thread a needle [an obscene euphemism for sexual intercourse

Emes - truth

Eppis - something undefinable, a "you-know-what"

Ess - eat

Faigelah - little bird (also used as a derogatory reference to a gay person)

Farbissenah - crabby

Farblonget - lost, confused

Farbrengen - a party, gathering

Farbrent - burning [zealous]

Fardrimmeled - dreaming, daydreaming

Farfallen - doomed

Farfel - broken up pieces of matzo

Farkakt [obscene] - shitty, fucked up

Farklempt - choked up

Farmished - mixed up, messed up

Farmutshet - Tired out

Farpatshket - Messed up

Farpitzed - dressed up

Farshimmeled - moldy

Farshlepte krenk - a long illness [an obnoxious person]

Farshlofener - sluggard

Farshluggine - beaten up, ratty

Farshnoshked - drunk

Farshtaitz - understand

Farshtunkene - stinky

Farshvist - sweaty

Fartootzed - over-dressed, overdone

Fartshadet - Distracted

Fin - Five-dollar bill

Fintzter un glitshik - dark and slippery [miserable]

Fis - foot

Flaishig - flesh; meat (as opposed to dairy)

Flanken - short ribs, often stewed

Fliegl - a wing

Forshpaiz - an appetizer

Fortz - a fart

Forvitz - Forward, a national Jewish newspaper

Frailikh - festive

Freidenker - a freethinker; atheist, secularist

Fress - eat like a glutton

Fresser - a glutton

Frosk - slap

Fumfen - to mumble

Futz - to fool around with

Gai - go

Galitzianer - a Jew from the Austro-Hungarian Empire

Ganef - a thief

Ganze makher - a big deal

Ganze megillah - the whole story (in detail)

Ganze mishpokha - the whole family

Gatkes - long underwear

Gazlan - a robber, swindler

Gazump - to cheat

Gedempte fleish - pot roast, brisket

Gederem - bowels

Gefilt croyt - stuffed cabbage

Gefilte fish - stuffed fish

Gehakhte tzoris - chopped up [terrible trouble]

Gehenem - Hell

Geherik; gehern - appropriate, to belong

Gelt - money

Gemish - a mixture

Genug - enough

Geshlekht - sex

Geshmakt - tasty

Geshrei - yell, shout

Get - a divorce decree

Gezunt - health

Gezuntheit - healthiness

Gilgul - Reincarnation

Glatt - smooth ["super" kosher]

Glatt azoy - just so [for no reason]

Glick - luck

Glitch - an error

Golakh - smooth [a monk]

Goldene Medina - the Golden Land

Golem - a soulless creature made of clay

Golus - Diaspora

Gorgl - throat

Gornisht - nothing

Gottenyu - oh, God

Goy -a nation [non Jews (pl. Goyim)]

Greener - a greenhorn

Greps - belch

Gribenes - crispy chicken skin

Gridzhen - gnaw or chew noisily [to nag]

Groysser putz [obscene] - big penis or big prick (derogatory or sarcastic)

Gunsel - in common usage, a hoodlum, armed gangster.

Haimish - homelike, comfortable

Hakhem - a wise person

Halevei - if only

Haskalah - the Enlightenment

Heizel - a whorehouse

Helzel - stuffed chicken necks

Himmel - heaven, sky

Hinten - rear [buttocks]

Holishkes - stuffed cabbage

Hondel - to haggle, make a deal

In mitn drinen - in the middle of

Kaddish - the Mourner's Prayer

Kaddishl - little Kaddish [son]

Kadokhes - chills and a fever [worthless]

Kak - crap

Kalba - a bitch

Kallah - a bride

Kaneh - an enema

Kapelye - a musical band

Kapore - a scapegoat

Kapote - a long coat

Kapsen - a cheapskate

Kasha varnishkes - buckwheat groats and bowtie pasta

Kemfer - a fighter, activist

Kenahora - keep away the evil eye

Kesubah - a marriage contract

Khalushes - terrible tasting

Khamalyeh - a punch, hard hit

Khamoyer du ainer - you ass

Khas v'khalilah - God forbid

Khas v'sholem - Heaven forbid

Khasana - a wedding

Khaver - a comrade [boyfriend in Modern Hebrew]

Khazzer - a pig; a glutton

Khazzerei - junk food

Khei kak [obscene] - human dung [nothing, infinitesimal, worthless, unimportant]

Kherem - excommunication

Khevraman - happy-go-lucky, irresponsible

Khnyok - a bigot

Khopper - a grabber [kidnapper who stole poor Jewish boys to conscript into Russian army]

Khoson - a groom

Khoyzek - Ridicule

Khoyzek makhn - make fun of

Khreyn - horseradish

Khuppah - a wedding canopy

Kibitz - small talk

Kibitzer - chatter

Kibosh - to cancel out, to dismiss

Kikhel - a crispy, concave, puffy, pastry coated with sugar

Kinde - a child

Kindelakh - little children

Kishke - stuffed derma

Kishkes - intestines

Kittel - a plain, white robe

Kitzel - tickle

Klafte - a bitch

Klainer gornisht - a little nothing

Klap - hit

Klap en kop - a hit on the head

Klezmer - a style of Eastern European Jewish music

Klutz - someone who is clumsy

K'nacker - a big shot; braggart

K'naidlakh - matzo balls

K'negedacker - a big shot, know-it-all, braggart

K'negedipl - the corner of a handerkerchief [a nest egg; euphemism for a hymen]

K'nish - dough filled with meat, potatoes, cheese, or other foods [obscene euphemism for vagina]

K'nobl - garlic

Kokhalein -cook alone [summer cottage with a kitchen]

Kokhleffel -cooking ladle [one who "stirs the pot" with rumors or gossip]

Kop - head

Kosher -proper, legal; foods allowed to be eaten by observant Jews

Krenk - sick

Kreplakh - a filled pastry, the Jewish version of wontons or ravioli.

Kugel - a baked pudding made with noodles or matzo

Kumsitz - come sit [a sing-a-long]

Kundis - a brat

Kurveh - a whore, prostitute

Kvell - to be proud of

Kvetch - to complain

Kvitsh - screech

Laidikgaier - an empty walker [an idler]

Landsman - a countryman

Landsmanshaft - a support organization of people from the same area

Latke - a potato pancake

Lekish - dummy, fool

Lemishke - an ineffectual person

Likht - light, holiday or Shabbos candles

Lipelakh - lips

Litvak - a Jew from Lithuania, Latvia, Poland, or Russia

Lokh in kop - a hole in the head

Lokhshen - noodle

Lox - smoked fish

Luftmensch - an airhead

Maidel - a maiden

Maikhel - a treat

Maise - a story, deed [obscene euphemism for intercourse]

Makeh - a plague, disease

Makhatonim - one's child's in-laws

Makhatonista - a mother-in-law

Makher - a big shot, influential person

Makhotin -a father-in-law

Mama loshen - mother's language [native tongue]

Mamaleh - little mother

Mamaliga - corn meal porridge

Mamzer - a bastard, disliked person, untrustworthy

Mandelbroyt - an almond cookie

Matzo - unleavened bread

Maven - an expert

Mazel tov - congratulations

Mazik - an impish child

Mazoola - money.

Megillah - a scroll [story]

Meichel - a treat

Mein tei'erer kaddishl - my dear little Kaddish

Mekhei'ya - that which makes life, resurrects [relief; joy]

Mekhieleh - forgiveness

Melamed - a teacher of young children

Mensch - a man [a good person]

Menschlich - to be a good person

Menschlikeit - the act of being a good person

Meshuga ahf toyt - crazy to death. [Really nuts.]

Meshugana - crazy

Meshugas - craziness

Metzie fon a ganef - a bargain from a thief. [a good deal, a steal]

Metzie'ah - a find [bargain]

Mezuma - cash

Mieskeit - one who is homely

Milkhik - dairy

Minyan - quorum of ten needed for communal prayer

Mishpokha - a family

Misnagdim - opponents [of the Chasidic sects]

Moyel - ritual circumciser

Moyl - mouth

Nafkeh - a prostitute

Nafkeh bais - a whorehouse

Nakhas - happiness

Nar - a fool

Narishkeit - foolishness

Nebbish - an ineffectual guy

Nebekh - a variation of nebbish

Nekhtiker tog - a night-like day [yesterday's news]

Nisht geferlakh - no big deal

Nishtikeit - a nothing

Nit gut - not good

Nokhshlepper - one who drag along after [a hanger-on]

Noodge - a pest

Nosh - a snack

Nosherai - snack food

Nu - so

Nusl - nuts

Oder a klop, oder a fortz. [obscene] - either a wallop or a fart. [Either too much or not enough.]

Oht azoy - as thus. [That's right! Just like that!]

Olam Ha'ba - the world to come

Ongebloozen - sulking

Ongepatchkt - overdressed, overdone

Ongeshtopf - overstuffed [loaded with money]

Onsaltn - to add salt [to sweet talk]

Ootz - tease, pester

Opgeflikt - suckered

Opgekrokhshene skhoyre - shoddy merchandise

Opgelozen - a careless dresser

Oy - alas

Oy gevalt - oh, how terrible

Oy vey iz mir - woe is me

Oy vey! - oh, no!

Oy, gotten - oh, my God [OMG!]

Oygn - Eyes

Oys shidukh - the engagement is over [The deal is off.]

Oysgemutshet - tired out

Oysoy hamokom - that place [a woman's privates]

Oyspishn - to urinate

Oystaam - tasteless [no flavor; no sense of style]

Oysvorf - outcast

Pahst - appropriate

Pai'is - side curls

Pareve (or parve) - neutral [neither dairy or meat]

Parnosseh - livelihood, income

Paskudne - disgusting, gross

Paskudnik - a scoundrel

Peklflaish - corned beef

Pesakh - Passover

Pesakhdik - appropriate for Passover

Petzeleh - little penis

Peyis - side curls worn by ultra-Orthodox men

Pintele - a point of light, spark of Jewishness

Pipek - navel, belly button

Pirge - a meat pie [obscene euphemism for vagina; similar to "pussy" in English]

Pishekhtz - urine

Pisher - a male infant, a little squirt, a nobody

Pishn - to urinate

Pitzel - wee, tiny (see petzeleh)

Plotz - explode, collapse

Potch - spank

Potch en tuchus - a spanking

Potch en punim - a slap on the face

Potchke - do too much, be obsessive

Prust - rough, coarse; socially unrefined

Prustak - a vulgar person

P'tcha - jellied calves feet

Pulke - a thigh [chicken leg]

Punim - a face

Pupik - navel, belly button

Purim - holiday based on Book of Esther

Pushka - a box or canister for collecting charity

Putz [obscene] - penis, derogatory term for a man

Putznasher [obscene] - cocksucker

Rebbe - master, teacher, usually a leader of a Chasidic sect or head of a Yeshiva

Rosh Hashanah - New Year

Rugelakh - a pastry

Saikhel - common sense

Schnapps - liquor

Sephard - Spain

Sephardi - a Jew from the Iberian Peninsula

Seudas mitzvah - a festive meal

Shabbos - the Sabbath

Shabbos goy - a non-Jew who helps with chores on Shabbos

Shadkhan - a matchmaker

Shaidim - demons

Shaigetz einer - a true non-Jew [an irreligious Jew]

Shaigitz - non-Jewish man

Shaina - beautiful

Shaina maidel - beautiful maiden

Shaina punim - beautiful face

Shaitl - a wig

Shamus - a detective

Shande - a shame, a public embarrassment

Shande un a kharpe - a shame and a disgrace

Shandhoyz - a house of shame [a whorehouse]

Shav - sorrel

Shavuos - Festival of Weeks

Shekhekheyanu - who has kept us alive [first word of a prayer of thanks]

Shemozzle - a brawl

Shidukh - an arranged match

Shikker - a drunk

Shiksa - non-Jewish woman

Shiva - seven days of mourning following a death

Shlang [obscene] - snake, serpent; a troublesome wife; penis

Shlekht veib - a bad wife [a shrew]

Shlemazel - a sad sack

Shlemiel - a slob, dork

Shlep - drag
Shlepper - a gofer; a hanger-on
Shlock - cheaply made goods
Shlockmeister - a purveyor of shoddy goods
Shlong [obscene] - a snake [a penis]
Shlub - a slob
Shluf - sleep
Shlump - messy, disheveled
Shmaltz - chicken fat [overly sentimental]
Shmatte - a rag
Shmear - a smear
Shmegegge - an idiot
Shmeikl - a smile, smooth talk
Shmeis - thrash [a rousing defeat]
Shmek'n - to smell
Shmendrick - a nincompoop
Shmo - a nobody,
Shmooze - idle chitchat
Shmuck [obscene] -penis [asshole]
Shmutz - dirt
Shnaps -hard liquor
Shnecken - a pastry
Shnook - a dork
Shnorrer - a beggar
Shnoz - a nose
Shokhad - a bribe, payola
Shokl - rhythmic rocking while praying
Shpilkes - nails [impatience]
Shpritz - a spray [seltzer]
Shrek - a horror
Shtadlan - a factotum [Court Jew]
Shtarker - someone strong
Shtetl - a small town

Shtiebl - a small synagogue

Shtik - a piece, an idiosyncrasy

Shtik drek [obscene] - piece of shit; shit-head

Shtik holtz - a piece of wood [a person with no personality]

Shtikl - a small piece

Shtipper - a brat

Shtunk - a stinker, a nasty person

Shtup - push, shove; vulgarism for sexual intercourse

Shul -a synagogue

Shund - trash

Shund-roman - a trashy novel

Shvakh - weak

Shvantz - penis

Shvartze - black [African-American]

Shvitz - sweat [steam bath]

Shvitzer - one who sweats [braggart]

Shvuntz - a coward

Simkha - a happy event

Sitzflaish - patience

Smeteneh - sour cream

Spiel - glib talk, play

Spiel zakh - a play thing [obscene euphemism for female privates]

Strashn - to threaten

Sukkos - Festival of Booths

Taam - taste

Taiglakh - small pieces of dough covered in honey

Takeh - untranslatable interjection similar to "really?" or "come on."

Takhlis - the heart of the matter

Tante - an aunt

Tateh - Dad

Tateh-Mama - father-mother [parents]

Tchotchke - a bauble

Tikhel - a kerchief

Toyten bankes - dead blood [blood letting]

Tref - non-kosher food

Tren - rip [screw, act of intercourse]

Trombenik - a phony

Tshepn - to pick on

Tu B'shvat - Jewish Arbor Day

Tuchus - buttocks, behind, fanny (ass)

Tuchus un a halb - a rear end and a half [a voluptuous woman]

Tuchuslecker [obscene] - a brown-noser, apple-polisher, ass-kisser

Tummler - an entertainer

Tzaddik - a righteous person

Tzainer - teeth

Tzatzke - a bauble (like tchatchka) [a cheap woman]

Tzibele - an onion

Tzimmes - a stew made often made with carrots prunes [overreacting]

Tzung - tongue

Tzuris - trouble

Tzutzik - an ambitious or energetic person

Umbatampt - tasteless

Umgelumpert - awkward, clumsy

Umglick -misfortune

Vern a tel - to be ruined [in shambles]

Vilde khei'a - a wild animal; refers to a brat

Vilder mensch - a wild person

Von zup zu nuslakh - from soup to nuts

Vontz - a bedbug [mischievous child]

Yakhneh - a coarse, loud-mouthed woman; a gossip; a slattern

Yakhsen - someone who has connections

Yarmulke - a skullcap, worn by observant Jews

Yasher koyekh - may your strength go forward [congratulations]

Yekke - a German Jew who is very prim and proper

Yenem - someone else

Yenemsville - wherever

Yenta - a gossip, busybody

Yentzen [obscene] - to fornicate, to whore, like "do" ("I did her") in English

Yeshiva - a school for traditional Jewish studies

Yeshiva bokher - a Yeshiva boy [a full-time student]

Yid - a Jew

Yiddene - a Jewish woman [wife]

Yiddishkeit - Jewishness

Yikhus - connections, influence

Yingele - a youngster

Yishka - Little Jesus

Yold - a yokel

Yom Kippur - Day of Atonement

Yontov - a holiday

Yortzeit - time of year [anniversary of a death]

Yungatch - a brat

Yutz - a stupid person

Zaftig - chubby

Zaide - grandfather

Zakh - thing [obscene euphemism for female privates]

Zetz - poke

Zieskeit - sweetie

Zoyere ugerke - sour cucumber [pickle]

Zup - Soup

II. Glossary of Sayings

A badkhan makht alle menschen frailikh un alain ligt er in drerd. A jester makes everyone laugh and he alone is miserable.

A behaimeh hot a langen tzung un ken nicht redden; der mensch hot a kurtzeh tzung un tor nisht reden. An animal has a long tongue and can't speak; a man has a short tongue and shouldn't speak.

A bokher a shadkhan, a moyd a bubbe - konnen nisht zein. A bachelor a matchmaker, a spinster a grandmother - these cannot be.

A brokh iz mir! I am cursed!

A brokh tzu dein lebn! A curse on your life!

A brokh tzu dein lebn, nish far dir degakht! A curse on your life, may it never happen to you!

A brokh tzu dir! A curse on you!

A brokh! Oh hell! Damn it!

A falsheh matba'ieh farliert men nit. A bad penny always turns up.

A fei'er zol im trefn. He should meet a fire! [He should burn up!]

A freint bekamt men umzist; a soyneh muz men zikh koyfn. A friend you get for nothing; an enemy has to be bought.

A freint darf men zikh koyfn; sonem krigt men umzist. A friend you have to buy; enemies you get for nothing.

A fremder nar iz a gleckhter; an aigener - a shand. A strange fool is a laughing stock; your own - an embarrassment.

A groys gesheft zol er hobn mit shroyre: vus er hot, zol men bei im nit fregn, un vos men fregt zol er nisht hobn. He should have a large store, and whatever people ask for he should not have, and what he does have should not be requested

A guten vet der shaink vit kalyeh makh, un a shlekhtne vet der bes-hamedresh nit fairkhtn. A good person won't be made bad by a tavern, and a bad one won't be reformed by the synagogue.

A gutter feint iz oft besser fun a bruder. A good friend is often better than a brother.

A halber emes iz a gantzer ligen. A half truth is a whole lie.

A hiltzener tzung zol er bakumn. He should grow a wooden tongue.

A kapn im in zain boykh. A cramp in his stomach!

A kapn in di gederem! A cramp in his bowels!

A katz meg oykh kuk'n oyfen kaisser. A cat can look at a king.

A kholaire ahf dir! A cholera on you!

A khissoren, di kalleh iz tzu shain. To a fault-finder, even the bride is too pretty.

A kholaire im zain bainer. A cholera in his bones.

A kindershe saikhel iz oykhet a saikhel. A child's wisdom is also wisdom.

A klap fargait, a vort bashtait. A blow passes, a word lingers.

A kleine veibeleh ken oykh hoben a groysse moyl. A small wife can also have a big mouth.

A ligner dark hoben a guten zekhron. A liar needs a good memory.

A ligner glaibt men nit, afileh az er zogt dem emes. No one believes a liar even when he tells the truth.

A ligner hert zikh zeine ligen azoy lang ein biz er glaibt zikh alain. A liar tells his story so often even he believes it.

A makeh ahf dir! A plague on you!

A makeh im zein boykh, a ruekh in zein tatns tate arein. A plague in his belly, a devil in his father's father.

A makeh in yenems oren iz nit shver trogen. Another's disease isn't hard to endure.

A meshuganer zol men oyshraibn, un im arainshraibn. They should free a madman, and lock him up instead.

A mise meshune ahf dir! An unnatural death on you!

A mol iz der refueh erger fun der makeh. Sometimes the cure is worse than the disease.

A nar bleibt a nar. A fool remains a fool.

A nar farlirt un a kluger gefint. A fool loses and a clever man finds.

A nar gait in bod arein un fargest zikh dos ponim opvashn. A fool goes to the baths and forgets to wash his face.

A nar gait tzvai mol dort, vu a kluger gait nit kain aintzik mol. A fool goes there [makes a bad decision twice, while a clever man doesn't go even once.

A nar git, a kluger nemt. A fool gives [advice], a wise man takes.

A nar ken a mol zogen a gleikh vort. Even a fool can sometimes say something clever.

A shadkhan must zein a ligner. A matchmaker must be a liar.

A shlekhte sholem iz besser vi a gutter krig. A bad peace is better than a good war.

A shlimazel falt oyfen ruken un tzeklapt zich dem noz. A shlimazel falls on his back and hits his nose.

A shprikhvort iz a vorvort. A proverb is a true word.

A shvartz yor ahf dir! A difficult year on you!

A tzaddik vos vais er iz a tzaddik iz kain tzaddik nit. A righteous man who knows he is righteous is not.

Abi gezunt - dos lebn ken men zikh alain nemen. Be well - you can kill yourself later.

Aider men zogt aroys s'vort, iz men a har; dernokh iz men a nar. Before you say a word you're a master; afterwards, you're a fool.

Ain mol a saikhel, dos tzvaiteh mol khain, dem dritten mol gil men in di tzain. The first time it's smart, the second time it's cute, the third time you get a sock in the teeth.

271

Ainer iz a ligen, tzvai iz ligens, drei iz politik.
One is a lie, two is a lie, three is politics.

Alle menschen muss zu machen, jeden tug a gentzen kak'n. Everyone has to take a crap every day.

Alle tzoris vos ikh hob oyf mein hartzn, zoln oysgain tzu zein kop. All problems I have in my heart, should go to his head.

Altzding lozst zikh oys mit a gevain. Everything ends in weeping.

Az der boykh iz laidik iz her moy'akh oylk laidik. When the stomach is empty, so is the brain.

Aus der putz shteyt, der seychel gait. When the prick stands up, reason departs.

Az di muter shreit oyfen kind, "Mamzer!" meg men ir gloyben. When a mother yells at her child, "Bastard!" you can believe her.

Az dos hartz iz ful, gai'en di oygen iber. When the heart is full, the eyes overflow.

Az es bashert ainem dertrunken tzu verren vert her dertrunken in a leffel vasser. If one is destined to drown, he will drown in a spoon of water.

Az ikh vel zein vi yener, ver vet zein vi ikh? If I would be like someone else, who would be like me?

Az men esst Shabbos kugel, iz men di gantzeh vokh zat. Eat kugel on the Sabbath and be full all week.

Az men muz, ken men. When one must, one can. [Necessity is the mother of invention.]

Az men ken nit iberharn dos shlekhteh, ken men dos guteh nit derleben. If you can't endure the bad, you won't live to witness the good.

Az meshiakh vet kumen, vellen alleh krankeh oysgehailt verren; nor a nar vet bleiben a nar. When the Messiah comes, all the sick will be healed; only a fool will stay a fool.

Az se brent, iz a fei'er. Where there's smoke, there's fire.

Azoy fil ritzinoyl zol er oystrink'n. He should drink too much castor oil.

Baide oygn deine zoln faln fon dein kop, khas vesholem. Both your eyes should fall out of your head, God forbid.

Bei a shadkhan iz nit kain miese kallah. According to a shadkhn, there's no homely bride.

Bei Mir Bist Du Shoen. By me, you are beautiful.

Besser tzu shtarben shtai'endik aider tzu leben oyf di k'ni. Better to die upright than to live on your knees.

Brenen zol er! He should burn (in hell)!

Brenen zolstu ahfn fei'er. You should burn in fire.

Der emes hot a sakh punimer. The truth has many faces.

Der mentsh trakht, un Got lakht. A man thinks and God laughs. [Man supposes and God disposes.]

Der vos hot nit fazukht bitterreh, vaist nit voz zies iz. One who has never tasted the bitter cannot know the sweet.

Der vos shveigt maint oykh epes. He who is silent still means something.

Di epeleh falt nit veit fun baimeleh. The apple doesn't fall far from the tree.

Di ergsteh rekhiles iz der emes. The worst libel is the truth.

Di gantzeh velt iz ful mit shaidim; treib zia khotsh fon zikh aroys. The whole world is full of demons; you just exorcise them out of yourself.

Di grub iz shoyn ofen un der mentsh tut nokh hofen. The grave is already open and man still hopes.

Di länger ein Blinder lebt, desto mehr sieht er. The longer a blind man lives, the more he sees.

Dos gehert nit tzu dir. That does not belong to you. [That's not your job. It is not your responsibility.]

Drai mir nit kain kop. Do not twist my head. [Stop pestering me.]

Du host a langer tzung. You have a long tongue. [You have a big mouth.]

Du zolst nor fortzn in drerd. You should only fart in the ground [in your grave].

Er frest vi a ferd. He eats like a horse.

Er hot kainmol nit eingefedemt. He has never threaded a needle [had sex].

Er muz zein a yamputz, veil ahf der yaboshe hob ikh nit gezen aza ainem. He must be a sea prick, because I have never seen such a prick on dry land.

Er zol altzting zen, un nit hobn mit vos tzu koyfn. He should see everything, but have nothing to buy it with.

Er zol hobn paroys makehs bashotn mit oybes kretz. He should have Pharaoh's plagues sprinkled with Job's scabies.

Er zol kak'n mit blit un mit aiter. He should crap blood and pus.

Es felt em der saikhel heioshor. He has no common sense.

Es iz a shande far di goyim. It's an embarrassment in front of the non-Jews.

Es iz a shande far di kinder. It's a shame in front of the children.

Es iz nit geshtoygen un nit gefloygen! It never rose and it never flew! [They ran it up the flag pole and no one saluted; i.e., it was a bullshit idea.]

Es vet helfen vi a toyten bankes. It will help like taking blood from a corpse.

Es zol dir dunern in boykh, vestu maien az s'iz a homon klaper. Your stomach will rumble so badly, you'll think it was Purim noisemaker.

Ess nisht di khale far a-moytze. Don't eat the challah before you've made the blessing.[Don't have sex before marriage.]

Ess, ess, mein kind. Eat, eat, my child.

Eyn umglik iz far im vainik. One misfortune is too few for him.

Far vus? For what, why?

Fardrai zikh dem kop. Turn your head [Drive yourself crazy.]

Faren dokter un aren beder zeinen nit kain soydes. There are no secrets from a doctor or a bathhouse attendant.

Farmakh dos moyl. Shut your mouth.

Farshporn zol er oyf shtain? Why should he bother to get up?

Finstere laid zol nor di mama oyf im zen.

Black sorrow is all that his mother should see of him.

Fon ain oks tzit men akin tzvai fellen nit arop. You can't get two skins from one ox.

Fon dein moyl in Gotz oyeren. From your mouth to God's ears.

Fon kin'ah vert sin'ah. Envy breeds hate.

Freg mikh b'kherem. Ask me when I'm excommunicated [How should I know?]

Frailikh zol zein. Be joyous.

Gai avek! Go away!

Gai gezunt. Go in health.

Gai gezunt un kum gezunt. Go in health and come in health.

Gai in drerd arein! Go to hell!

Gai kak'n in dem yam. Go shit in the ocean. [Get lost.]

Gai kak'n ahfen yam! Go shit on the sea. [Get lost.]

Gai plotz! Go blow up!

Gai shlog dein kop in vant. Go bang your head on the wall.

Gai shlufn. Go to sleep.

Gai shoyn, gai! Go away already!

Gai strashe di vantzn! Go threaten the bedbugs! [You don't scare me!].

Gai tren zikh. [obscene] Go fuck yourself.

Genug iz genug. Enough is enough.

Gornisht helfen. Nothing helps; it makes no difference.

Got hat eine Welt voller kleiner Weltchen ershaffen. God created one world full of small worlds.

Got zol im bentshn mit drei mentshn: ainer zol im haltn, der tzvaiter zol im shpaltn un der driter zol im ba'haltn. God should bless him with three people: one should grab him, the second should stab him, and the third should hide him.

Got zol gebn, er zol hobn altzding vos zein hartz glist, nor er zol zein gelaimt oyf alle eivers un nit kenen rirn mit der tzung. God should bestow him with everything his heart desires, but he should be a quadriplegic and not be able to use his tongue.

Got zol oyf im onshik'n fin di tzen makehs di beste. God should visit upon him the best of the Ten Plagues.

Hak mir nit kein tsheinik. Don't knock my teakettle. [Don't pester me.]

Heng dikh oyf a tzikershtrikl vestu hobn a zisn toyt. Hang yourself with a sugar rope and you'll have a sweet death.

Hindert heizer zol er hobn, in yeder hoyz a hindert tzimern, in yeder tzimer tzvonsik betn un kadukhes zol im varfn fin ain bet in der tzvaiter. A hundred houses he should have, in every house a hundred rooms and in every room twenty beds, and a delirious fever should drive him from bed to bed.

Ikh darf zikh oyspishn. I have to take a leak.

Ikh faif ahf dir! I whistle on you! [I wash my hands of you.]

Ikh hob dikh in bod! I'll have you in the bath! [Watch your back. I'll get you when you least expect it.]

Ikh hob dikh in drerd! I'll have you in hell. [To hell with you!]

Ikh hob dir! I'll have you! [I know what you're up to. Drop dead!]

Ikh hob es in drerd! To hell with it!

Ikh hob im in bod! I'll have him in the bath! [He better watch his back!]

Ikh hob im in drerd! I'll have him in hell. [To hell with him!]

In di zumerdike teg zol er zitzn shive, un in di vinterdike nekht zikh reisn ahf di tzain. On summer days he should mourn, and on wintry nights, he should torture himself.

In mitn drinen. In the middle of it all.

Iz nisht kosher. It's not appropriate.

Kak im on. (obscene) Crap on him! [The hell with him!]

Kak zikh oys! (obscene) Go take a shit for yourself!

Khamoyer du ainer! You blockhead! You dope, you ass.

Khasene hobn zol er mit di malekh hamoves tokhter. He should marry the daughter of the Angel of Death.

Kom vos er krikht. Come whatever, he crawls. [He's a slowpoke.]

Kush in toches arein! (Obscene) Kiss my ass!

Kush mir in toches! Kiss my ass!

Laiben ahf dein kop. Life on your head. [Good job! Nice work!]

Lakhn zol er mit yashtherkes. He should laugh with lizards. [Lizards aren't known for laughing, so he should never laugh or be happy again.]

Lig in drerd! Lie in the ground! [Bury yourself! Get lost! Drop dead!]

Lig in drerd un bak beygl. Lie in the ground and bake bagels! [You can't if you're dead.]

Loz im gai'n. Let them go.

Loz mikh tzu ruh! Leave me in quiet. [Leave me alone!]

Melokheh bez deigeh. To have a trade is to be free of worry.

Men ken brekhn. It can make you vomit.

Meshuga zol er vern un arumloyfn iber di gasn. He should go nuts and run around through the streets.

Migulgl zol er vern in a hengleihter, by tog zol er hengen, un bei nakht zol er brenen. He should be transformed into a chandelier: by day he should hang, and by night he should burn.

Nem on a fuln moyl vaser! Fill up your mouth with water. [Keep your mouth shut.]

Nem zikh a vane! Take a bath! [Go jump in the lake!]

Nisht gerferalakh. Not dangerous. [Don't worry about it; it's nothing.]

Nit dos iz shain, vos iz shain, nor dos, vos es gefelt. Beautiful is not what is beautiful, but what one likes. [Beauty is in the eye of the beholder.]

Nit gedeiget. Not to worry. [No worries! Everything's great.]

Nit kain entfer iz oykh an entfer. No answer is also an answer.

Nokh di khuppah iz shpet di kharoteh. After the khuppah, it's too late for regrets.

Odem yesode meofe vesofe leofe - beyno-lveyno iz gut a trink bronfn. A man comes from the dust and in the dust he will end - in the meantime it is good to drink whiskey.

Oder es helft nit oder men darf es nit. Either it doesn't help or you don't need it.

Oy, ikh darf zikh oyspishn - geferlekh! Boy, do I need to take a leak something fierce!

Oyf der shukh pahst, kenst im trogen. If the shoe fits, wear it.

Oyf drei zakhen shtait di velt: oyf gelt, oyf gelt, oyf gelt. The world stands on three things: money, money, money.

Oyf doktoyrim zol er dos avekgebn. He should give it (his money) all away to doctors.

Oyf vemens vogen me zitzt, zingt men dem lied. On whoever's wagon you're sitting, that's whose tune you're singing. [He who pays the piper picks the tune.]

Oyskrenk'n zol er dus mame's milakh. He should get so sick as to cough up his mother's milk.

Pahst nisht. It's not appropriate.

Parnosseh iz a refueh tzu alleh krenk. A good livelihood cures all ills.

Potch on tuchus. Give a spanking.

Reden iz shver un shveigen kenmen nit. Speech is difficult, but silence impossible.

Reden iz zilber, shveigen iz gold. Speech is silver, silence is golden.

Shainkeit fargait, khokhme bashteit. Beauty fades, wisdom stays.

Shtainer ahf zeine bainer. Stones on his bones.

Shtainer zol zi hobn, nit kain kinder. Stones she should have, and not children.

Shtup es in toches! (Obscene) Shove [or stick] it up your rear [ass]!

Trink'n zoln im piavkes. Leeches should drink him dry.

Tuchus ahfen tish! Ass on the table! [Put up or shut up! Let's conclude this!]

Tzen shifn mit gold zol er farmorgn, un dos gantze gelt zol er farkrenk'n. Ten ships of gold should be his and the money should only make him sick.

Umglik binds tzunoyf. Misfortune binds together. [Misery loves company.]

Ven dos volt nit geven mein meshuganer, volt ikh oykh gelakht! If he were not my madman, [if he were not related to me], I'd laugh at him, too.

Ven me lakht ze'en alleh; ven me vaint zet kainer nisht. When you laugh, all see; when you cry, no one sees.

Ven men darf hoben moy'akh, helft nit kain koy'akh. When you need brains, brawn won't help.

Ven si farleshen zikh di likht, haiben on tantzen di meiz. When the lights go out, the mice dance. [When the cat's away, the mice will play.]

Ver filt zikh, der meynt zikh. Who feels guilty, feels responsible.

Vi Iz Ei'er Nomen? What is your name?

Vi tzu derleb ikh im shoyn tzu bagrobn. I should outlive him long enough to bury him.

Vifil yor er iz gegangn oyf di fis zol er gain ahf di hent un di iberike zol er zikh sharn oyf di hinten. As many years as he has walked on his feet, he should walk on his hands, and for the rest of the time he should crawl along on his ass.

Vilst a kopeh in mehkieleh arein? Do you want a kick in the pardon-the-expression?

Vilst essn bei mir kreplakh? Do you want to eat kreplakh with me? [Are you looking for a knuckle sandwich?]

Vo den? What then?

Vos makht a Yid? What makes a Jew? [What's going on? How are you doing?]

Vos makht du? What makes you? [How are you?]

Vos mer gevart, mer genart. He who hesitates is lost.

Yeder hartz hot soydes. Every heart has secrets.

Yeder mentsh iz oyf zikh alain blind. Every man is blind to his own faults.

Zai nit kain Veizoso! Don't be Veizoso [one of Haman's sons]! [Don't be a fool!]

Zai nit meshuga. Don't be crazy.

Zaltz im in di oygn, feffer im in di noz. Throw salt in his eyes, pepper in his nose.

Zein mazl zol im leihtn vi di levone in sof khoydesh. His luck should be as bright as a new moon.

Zi iz geven a kurveh in di mames boykh. She was a whore in her mother's stomach.

Zingn ken ikh nit, ober a maven bin ikh. I can't sing, but I'm an expert. [Those who can, do; those who can't, criticize.]

Zol di markh oprinen fon deine bainer. Your bones should be drained of marrow.

Zol dikh kapn beim boykh. You should get a stomach cramp.

Zol dir klapn in kop. It should bang in your head. [May it only happen to you like to me.]

Zol er brenem in gehenem. He should burn in hell.

Zol er hobn a kapn im di kishkes. He should have a cramp in his guts.

Zol er krenken un gedenken. He should suffer and remember.

Zol er lebn - oder nit lang. He should live - but not long.

Zol er lebn bis hundert un tzvantzik yor - on a kop. He should live to 120 years - without a head.

Zol er tzebrekhen a fis. He should break a leg.

Zol er vern dershtikt. He should be strangled.

Zol er vern gesharget. He should be murdered.

Zol es im onkumn vos ikh vintzh im, khotsh a helft, khotsh halb, khotsh a tzent khailik. What I wish on him should come true, most, even half, even just ten percent.

Zol vaks tzibeles fon dein pupik. Onions should grow from your bellybutton.

Zolst farlirn alle tzainer akhutz ainem, un der zol dir vai ton. You should lose all your teeth except one, and that one should ache!

Zolst farlirn alle deine tzainer akhutz ainer, un in dem zolst hobn a shreklikher tzainvaitik.

You should lose all your teeth but one, and you should have a terrible toothache in it.

Zolst habn a ziser toyt - a vagon mit tzuker zol dir iberforn. You should have a sweet death - a wagon full of sugar should run you over.

Zolst habn a zun vos men ruft nokh dir - un in gikhn. You should have a son named for you - and soon. [Ashkenazi Jews name their children after someone who is deceased.]

Zolst tze brekhn alle deine bainer az oft mol vi di brekhtz di aseres hadibres. You should break your bones as often as you break the Ten Commandments.

Bibliography

Allen, Woody. The Insanity Defense: The Complete Prose. (New York, NY: Random House, 2007).

Mere Anarchy. (New York, NY: Random House, 2007).

Ayto, John, & Ian Crofton. Brewer's Dictionary of Modern Phrase and Fable. (New York, NY: Sterling Publishing Co., 2006).

Blech, Rabbi Benjamin. Complete Idiot's Guide to Learning Yiddish. (New York, NY: Alpha, 2002).

Emmes, Yetta. Drek!: The Real Yiddish Your Bubbe Never Taught You. (New York, NY: Plume, 1998).

Epstein, Lita. If You Can't Say Anything Nice, Say It in Yiddish: The Book of Yiddish Insultz and Curses. (New York, NY:Citadel Press, 2006).

Franzos, Karl Emil. Michael Mitchell, translator. Leib Weihnachtzkuchen and His Child. (Ariadne Press, 2005; originally published 1896)

Garrett, Leah: "Al Jaffee Explains How Mad Magazine Made American Humor Jewish," Forward, February 21, 2016. (forward.com/culture/yiddish-culture/333672/al-

jaffee-explains-how-mad-magazine-made-
american-humor-jewish/)

Kogos, Fred. From Shmear to Eternity: The
Only Book of Yiddish You'll Ever Need. (New
York, NY:Citadel Press, 2006).
The Dictionary Of Yiddish Slang and
Idioms. (New York, NY: Citadel, 2002).
The Dictionary Of Popular Yiddish
Words, Phrases And Proverbs. (New York, NY:
Citadel, 1997).

Loeffler, James. "Di Rusishe Progresiv
Muzikal Yunyon No. 1 Fun Amerike: The First
Klezmer Union In America - Klezmer: History
And Culture," Judaism. (Winter, 1998).

Peer, Janet. Yiddish for Dogs. (New York,
NY: Hyperion, 2007).

Rosten, Leo. Hooray for Yiddish! (New
York, NY: Simon & Schuster, 1982).
The Joys of Yiddish. (New York, NY:
McGraw Hill, 1968).The New Joys of Yiddish.
revised by Lawrence Bush. (New York, NY:
Three Rivers Press, 2001)

Samuel, Maurice. In Praise of Yiddish.
(New York, NY: Cowles Book Company, 1971).

Sinclair, Julian. Let's Schmooze: Jewish
Words Today. (London: Continuum, 2007).

Singer, Joel. May You …! How to Curse in Yiddish. (New York, NY: Ballantine, 1977).

Stevens, Payson R., Charles M. Levine, & Sol Steinmetz. Meshuggenary: Celebrating the World of Yiddish. (New York, NY: Simon & Schuster, 2002).

Stutchkoff, Nahum: Thesaurus of the Yiddish Language (as quoted in http://yiddishradioproject.org/exhibitz/stutchkoff/curses.php3)

Vincent, Isabel. Bodies and Souls: The Tragic Plight of Three Jewish Women Forced into Prostitution in the Americas. (New York, NY: William Morrow, 2005).

Weiner, Ellis and Barbara Davilman. Yiddish with George and Laura. (New York, NY: Little, Brown, 2006).

Weinreich, Uriel. Modern English-Yiddish, Yiddish-English Dictionary. (New York, NY: Schocken Books, 1977).

Wex, Michael. Born to Kvetch: Yiddish Language and Culture in All of Its Moods. (New York, NY: Harper Perennial, 2006).
Just Say Nu: Yiddish for Every Occasion (When English Just Won't Do). (New York, NY: St. Martin's Press, 2007).

answers.yahoo.com

ask.com

ariga.com/yiddish.shtml

bnaimitzvahguide.com/common.yiddish.terms.php

cjh.org

dictionary.reference.com

etymonline.com

forward.com

hebrew4christians.com/Glossary/Yiddish_Words/yiddish_words.html

imbd.com

jewishcurrents.org/yiddish-curses-for-republican-jews

jewish-languages.org

jewishvirtuallibrary.org

jewishworldreview.com

juf.org

koshernosh.com/dictiona.htm

lexicool.com/ectaco-online-dictionary.asp

lingvozone.com/Yiddish

mahamatzav.com

myjewishlearning.com

mysite.verizon.net/jialpert/Yiddish/Glossary.htm

newyorker.com/humor/daily-shouts/yiddish-curses-for-republican-jews

pass.to/glossary

tau.ac.il/~itamarez/works/papers/papers/lngconfl.htm

the-yiddish-world-of-michael-wex.com

uta.fi/FAST/US1/yidgloss.html

wikipedia.org

wordcraft.infopop.cc
worldwidewords.org/weirdwords/
yiddishdictionaryonline.com
yiddishisms.com
yivo.com
youtube.com

And sixty years of reading Mad Magazine